The
STORY OF THE
GREAT
BRITISH
BAKE OFF

ANITA SINGH is a journalist who has covered television, film and culture for nearly 20 years, including a decade as arts and entertainment editor for *The Daily Telegraph*. She lives in London with her husband and two children. She really loves cake.

The

STORY OF THE
GREAT
BRITISH
BAKE OFF

ANITA SINGH

First published in the UK in 2017 by Anima,
an imprint of Head of Zeus Ltd.

9 7 5 3 1 2 4 6 8

A CIP catalogue record for this book is available
from the British Library.

ISBN (HB) 9781786694430
ISBN (E) 9781786694423

Design and typesetting by Saffron Stocker and Adrian McLaughlin
Printed and bound in Italy by L.E.G.O. S.p.A.

Head of Zeus Ltd
First Floor East
5–8 Hardwick Street
London EC1R 4RG
WWW.HEADOFZEUS.COM

CONTENTS

1

THE
SHOW

'It's just a show about twelve normal, wonderful people trying to do something sincerely and well.'

Take one tent. Fill with twelve amateur bakers. Garnish with one venerable cookery writer, one blue-eyed bread-maker, and two mischievous presenters. Mix in some triumphs, disasters and soggy bottoms. Finally, sprinkle with a little television magic. And there you have the recipe for the most popular show of modern times.

When *The Great British Bake Off* made its debut one Tuesday night in August 2010 it had all the makings of a modest hit. But nobody – not the programme-makers, not the executives who commissioned it, and certainly not those first contestants – could have predicted what was to come.

Here was a show in which the biggest weekly drama was whether or not a sponge cake would sink in the middle. An elimination contest in which the contestants didn't want their rivals to be eliminated, and the grand prize was a cake stand. A display of showstoppers by some of the least showy people ever to appear on the telly. An hour of watching strangers kneeling on the floor and peering anxiously into ovens. And oh, how we loved it.

As the hit show settles into its new home on Channel 4, with a fresh line-up of presenters – Paul Hollywood remaining at the helm, aided by the magisterial Prue Leith and the quirky double act of Sandi Toksvig and Noel Fielding – that very first series seems a long time ago. We've had our fair share of drama. When it was announced that *The Great British Bake Off* was upping sticks, breaking up the on-screen team viewers knew and had come to love, the news knocked David Cameron's resignation off the front pages and prompted a period of national mourning. A few weeks later, the grand final of the very last BBC series became the most-watched programme on British television since the closing ceremony of the London 2012 Olympics.

How had a gentle baking show become a global phenomenon?

When *Bake Off* came along, it was a programme like no other. The boardroom backstabbing of *The Apprentice*, ritual humiliations of *The X Factor* and petty conflicts of *Big Brother* were entirely absent, as were the fame-hungry wannabes who populated them. Nobody punches the air when they win a challenge – instead, in that terribly British way, they're faintly embarrassed to be singled out for praise. Nobody is giving it 110 per cent (bakers are good at maths). Nobody has 'wanted this my whole life' despite only being twenty-

three. Nobody has been on 'an amazing journey' (well, Nadiya Hussain might have said that, but we'll let her off because in her case it's true). They are just a bunch of ordinary people who really love to bake.

Their crises are small – 'catastrophe in a cupcake' is how the programme-makers describe it – but that reflects the everyday lives of the audience more closely than any soap opera. What really sets the show apart, though, is its kindness. The bakers help and support one another; the tears when a contestant leaves each week are genuine. They are amateurs, doing their very best, and we are there to will them on.

BAKE OFF STATS

Broadcast in over 200 countries

*

Sold as a format in 26 territories, including the USA, France, Australia and Russia

*

Won over 12 awards, including 3 BAFTAS and 1 National Television Award

*

Became the most watched show in the UK for the past 2 years

*

Grown its fan base from 2 million to 15.9 million

Britain was a funny old place in the summer of 2010. The old certainties had gone. Austerity was kicking in. The country had a coalition government, ensuring that, whatever your political persuasion, you probably felt short-changed. The Labour Party had gone all Cain and Abel with the Miliband brothers. A volcanic ash cloud had ruined people's holidays. The nation appeared to be in the grip of a sense of humour failure. There was only one constant in an ever-changing world: England had been knocked out of the World Cup. The time was right for a show in which the words 'Great' and 'Britain' could be uttered without a vague sense of awkwardness. Something feel good. The television equivalent of a cup of tea and a lovely slice of cake.

Enter Love Productions, a television company set up in 2004 by Anna Beattie and Richard McKerrow. The couple had originally met at Channel 4 and decided to set up on their own. Love soon gained notoriety for bringing an entertainment slant to tough subjects normally reserved for documentaries: homelessness (*Famous, Rich and Homeless*, where tennis start Annabel Croft slept rough with the Marquess of Blandford) and teen pregnancy (*The Baby Borrowers*, where young couples took loan of strangers' babies). It was a formula that worked well, earning the company a string of commissions from the BBC and Channel 4.

The company came up with the idea of a baking show based on a village fête cake competition. Despite the fact that they came up with this idea as early as 2004, Beattie and McKerrow spent four years trying to interest broadcasters in it. 'We just kept on with it because we knew it was a good idea,' Beattie has said. And in 2009, the BBC decided to take a punt on the series.

In many ways *Bake Off* was a departure from the gritty issues Love Productions was used to tackling. Here was a show that delivered the 1950s fantasy: a Cath Kidston and Emma Bridgewater world of village fêtes and vicars, afternoon tea and grand country piles, England's pastures green, jam and Jerusalem, Midsomer without the murders. A place where no one swears and everyone wears a pinny.

*

The original pitch resembled the show that the nation has taken to its heart. It was always intended to be as much about the people as the recipes. The production company described it in their earliest notes as 'like a *Spellbound* for baking' (a reference to the 2002 documentary which took a hitherto unfashionable subject – US children's spelling bees – and made it gripping by getting the audience emotionally invested in the stories of the individual contestants).

The Great British Bake Off was set out to be an entertainment show with a similar documentary feel. The series would 'reach out to all corners of Britain to find the most passionate bakers with the best stories.' As that first pitch explained, 'It's also a very entertaining way of looking at the cultural make-up of Britain today. *Panorama* might examine the multicultural nature of Britain through statistics, electoral registers, examinations of disharmony in local communities, etc, but we do it by pitting a Victoria sponge against a Jamaican gingerbread and a very postmodern violet cupcake.' It was described as 'a timely piece of escapism and aspiration. Much as watching all that blue sky on *A Place in the Sun* makes us feel better, baking is feel good. It's pretty, it's cosy, it's even funny. It's just the thing for these miserable times. In fact it's even proven that baking does flourish when people are feeling the pinch financially. So bring on the British Bakers. . .'

The programme-makers promised a mix of social and ethnic backgrounds, single dads, yummy mummies and wily pensioners. But some suggestions would not make the final cut. The prize could be a cookbook contract or the chance of a recipe in print – publishers would be sounded out about the possibility. The judging panel might feature a WI grandee or buyer for a major supermarket. Although they were keen to travel around the country, Love thought the final might take place in London, with members of the public invited to taste the bakes. 'At one point there was talk of filming hopefuls queuing around the block at the auditions,' recalls one person involved in the initial brainstorming. 'A sort of *X Factor* with cupcakes.'

The format mixed two of the most popular TV genres: cookery shows and elimination contests. You know the elimination drill – start with a dozen or so contestants, set them a series of challenges and boot off the weakest every week until three finalists remain. It had worked for singers (*The X Factor*), dancers (*Strictly*), and entertainers hoping for a slot on Loose Women (*I'm A Celebrity*). But could it work for bakers? These shows need jeopardy. And while, on paper, cake-making and biscuit-icing may seem unlikely sources of tension, in the end they proved

they were. Will those cakes rise? Will that icing set? And will those biscuits stack into a foot-high replica of the moon landing?

*

Until Nigella Lawson arrived on the scene, casting lascivious glances at profiteroles and flirting with peanut butter cheesecake, baking was not in fashion. The landscape of television food shows in the 2000s owed much to Jamie Oliver, whose bish-bash-bosh method – chuck in a bit of this, shake it about a bit, and job's a good 'un – had made cooking seem fun, easy and the sort of thing you could knock together with your mates while clutching a bottle of lager and sliding down the bannister to Toploader. Sensing the shift, the BBC launched *Saturday Kitchen* in 2002, with a similarly laidback vibe and an emphasis on food you could whizz up without too much effort. Weighing out ingredients and waiting patiently for some dough to prove seemed dull by comparison.

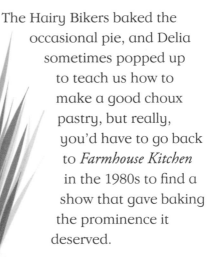

The Hairy Bikers baked the occasional pie, and Delia sometimes popped up to teach us how to make a good choux pastry, but really, you'd have to go back to *Farmhouse Kitchen* in the 1980s to find a show that gave baking the prominence it deserved.

And baking was always presented in the same

style. 'Previously, any show that involved baking would have someone standing behind a table with everything weighed out in front of them, à la Delia Smith, and they would tip things into a large bowl and put it all together. And it was professional, and always came out looking good,' says food writer Rose Prince.

The decade before *Bake Off* gave us cooking shows where food really wasn't the point: *Hell's Kitchen*, which we watched for Gordon Ramsay's volcanic rages; *Come Dine With Me*, in which the amount of fun we had was in direct proportion to how terrible the dishes were. And then there was *MasterChef*, once a ponderous hour in the company of Loyd Grossman, now revived with the blokey pairing of John Torode and Gregg Wallace.

The BBC reckoned their new baking show was sufficiently different to merit its own weekly slot and eventually signed it up. The launch was set in motion, with cautious hopes and expectations on all sides. The first press release described it as a show that would 'tell the history of Britain through baking', which feels a somewhat modest promise for a show that would become one of the most celebrated on TV.

2

THE FRONT OF HOUSE

The search for the judges began with a brief to find baking experts who were 'credible, passionate and likeable'. Ideally one of them would be a professional baker, but it wasn't a necessity. It involved looking for cooks who had written bestselling books, finding names on the BBC Food website, identifying people who stood out from UKTV Food talent lists, talking to respected food journalists – people who had a platform and were good on camera. There was an extensive longlist, including Jane Asher, Rachel Allen and Clarissa Dickson-Wright. And then there was Mary.

For many people below the age of forty, Mary Berry was not a well-known name. A *Times* television previewer, setting out the first episode, explained to readers that the judge was 'a lovely posh lady called Mary Berry'. Even some of the bakers were unfamiliar with her. Johnny Shepherd from series one 'had no idea who Mary was – she was of a different generation. It's only since the show that she's gone back into the mainstream and appealed to people from 5 to 105.' Simon Blackwell, persuaded to apply by his wife and not much of a TV-watcher, turned up to the series two auditions and asked a researcher before heading in to see Mary and Paul: 'What are their names?'

Mary was drifting happily into semi-retirement in 2009 after a lifetime as a cookery writer, with plans to improve her tennis game and concentrate on the garden. Her CV had just the right sort of retro feel to chime with *Bake Off*. A Cordon Bleu-trained cook, she started out as an editor of *Housewife* magazine ('For Go-Ahead Young Wives!') in the 1960s and then wrote two 1970s bestsellers, *The Hamlyn All Colour Cookbook* and *The Complete Book of Freezer Cooking*, the cover of the latter featuring a Granny Smith and a strawberry in a faintly suggestive embrace, so Seventies in its styling that it could have graced a Roxy Music album cover. She made regular appearances on TV in the 1970s and 1980s, including the Judith Chalmers' daytime show, *Afternoon Plus*, but she was primarily known for her books. There was only space for one female TV cook with sensible hair and a foolproof recipe for vol-au-vents, and Delia Smith had bagged it. Mary concentrated on writing, and cakes were her thing.

She recorded a 1996 series, *Mary Berry's Ultimate Cakes*, which proved popular. But times were changing in TV-land. One of the most popular cooking shows of the time was *Ready Steady Cook*, a sort of gameshow in which members of the public brought in a random selection of ingredients and two chefs competed to make the least awful meal out of them. Then, with the arrival of Jamie and Nigella, food shows became another form of entertainment, usually watched by people sitting in front of the TV with a takeaway.

So Mary had stepped aside, until in 2009 her agent called to say that a production company had been in touch with an idea for a village fête-style cake competition. 'I immediately thought, well, that's right up my street, because if there's one thing I know about then it is cakes,' she wrote in her memoir. She has described her style as 'quiet, gentle, detailed. No shouting, no dramas. I don't like all that.' It could be a description of *Bake Off* itself.

But although she was one of the first people that Love met, Mary was far from a dead cert. As Richard McKerrow later recalled: 'In all honesty, we didn't have great expectations necessarily.'

Then they watched her screen test. 'We put the tape in and it was one of those slam dunk moments. Oh my God, the camera loved her.'

By Mary's admission, bread was not her forte, so it made sense for the second judge to have bread-making skills as this was to be a big component of the show. This search was trickier and Love ended up with a longer list of final favourites. Dan Lepard, Tom Herbert of The Fabulous Baker Brothers, and chefs Galton Blackiston and Nigel Haworth were all considered. Enter the silver fox.

Paul Hollywood was a baker by trade, having worked his way up from his dad's bakery to become the youngest head baker at The Dorchester. During a stint at a hotel in Cyprus, where he met his wife, Alexandra, a production company doing a food show on the island asked him to present one of the items. Back in the UK he dabbled in TV, pairing up with James Martin for one show, but he remained relatively unknown. The stars aligned, though, as *Bake Off* brainstorming was under way, and it was mentioned that he had once appeared with Mary on a cable channel. He screen-tested, and it went like a dream, impressing the production company with his ease at explaining the technical skills involved in bread-making.

At the time, Paul was running his own one-man bakery business, doing the deliveries himself in a ten-year-old van. Probably his biggest brush with fame had been inventing Britain's most expensive loaf, a £15 Roquefort-and-almond sourdough, available only at Harrods.

Then, out of the blue, he got a call about *Bake Off*. 'They said I'd be working with an older person. That's all I was told. And I walked into an office in London and Mary was sitting there and she goes, "Oh! I knew it was you!",' he recalled in his appearance on *Desert Island Discs*. 'I go up and give her a hug and it was just one of those things; we just hit it off straight away.'

They complemented each other perfectly: Mary with her schoolmistress air and perfect Home Counties diction, Paul with the Wirral accent and alpha male tendencies. They didn't always come to easy decisions: in series one, they took nearly five hours to deliberate over whether Miranda Gore Browne should go through (Mel: 'It was like waiting for a new pope.'). But there was never a cross word between them. 'We think in sync,' Paul has said. 'We always know exactly what we're looking for. We've got closer and closer. I never pass her house without calling her. I love her to pieces. It's a sort of mother–son thing going on.'

The production company saw the chemistry between them right from that initial screen test. They adored the Mary-and-Paul partnership. And Mary loved Paul. It was a perfect pairing. Finding the non-cooking presenters was a slightly different challenge, as it was not always obvious what they were looking for.

Mel Giedroyc and Sue Perkins met as teenagers in their first term at Cambridge University, on the sticky carpet of the Footlights comedy club. They formed a double act after graduation, performing on the fringe circuit and landing a job as gag writers for Dawn French and Jennifer Saunders. Their big break came in 1997 hosting a slightly insane daytime show on Channel 4 called *Light Lunch*. It involved the pair interviewing celebrities while all of them ate lunch (crab risotto with Kylie, jambalaya with

Twiggy). This turned out to be a bit of a design flaw as everyone had to keep pausing to chew their food between sentences. But it was a laugh, and proved how brilliantly the pair could ad lib. They became household names thanks to enjoyably daft ads for Kingsmill bread, but by the mid-2000s their popularity had waned. Mel took time off to have children; Sue had a period in the TV wilderness, but later underwent a career revival in the *Supersizers* series that she starred in with Giles Coren. It involved living for a week in a different period in history (Edwardian, Victorian, Seventies) and eatingmeals of the time. In short, the Mel and Sue CV can be boiled down to: Being Funny Around Food. So who better to host *Bake Off*? Other names were under consideration in the early stages, but then the BBC hit on the idea of hiring Sue. She had impressed them with her work on *Supersizers*, and by winning the 2008 BBC2 show *Maestro* which culminated in her conducting an orchestra at the Proms. When Sue was approached about *Bake Off*, she wrote in her autobiography that she worried the show would be like watching paint dry, 'except worse, because after paint's dry you can at least hang pictures on it and sit back and admire it, whereas with a cake you just eat it and then feel awful about yourself'. She thought of turning it down, but was swayed by the prospect of being reunited with her old mucker

Mel. BBC2 controller Janice Hadlow, a fan of *Light Lunch*, had the inspired thought of bringing them back together.

A show insider said: 'Them saying "yes" was a huge relief.' And when the four presenters and judges got together, it worked perfectly. It helped that Sue was a fan of Paul's 'big arms' from his days on UKTV Food.

Mel had also been relieved when the offer came in. After a long period out of work she really needed the money. She has been quoted as saying that in those early days of *Bake Off*, 'all I thought was "mortgage, mortgage, mortgage".'

Mel didn't expect the show to be a hit either – speaking on Radio 2 this year, she admitted: 'When we filmed series one, hand on heart, I was phoning up Sue and saying, "Don't worry, mate, no one's going to watch this, it is a bit twee, we're in a marquee with some bunting, this could have quite negative results for us, but no one's going to see it. We're paying off the mortgage, it's a one-series wonder." And then this thing happened. It was utterly, utterly bizarre.'

Even after filming the first series, she wasn't confident it would be re-commissioned. In fact, she was so sure it wouldn't be back again that she purloined an expensive bouquet of fake flowers that had adorned the tent. They now have pride of place in her kitchen.

If you ask the bakers from the first seven series about some of their fondest memories of the show, they talk about Mel and Sue.

Right from the very first episode, they made the tent feel like home and were on hand to offer a comforting hug or a terrible pun, as the situation demanded. 'Our job is very simple. Mary

and Paul do a little judging, and Mel and I make sure the bakers are all right,' is how Sue described it. But only skilled presenters can make a job like this look easy, and they managed the tricky task of hosting the show without overpowering it. They struck the perfect balance between humour and seriousness, reminding the bakers that it's only a cake, while acknowledging that it's also so much more than a cake.

'They were there to chat, to make it a nice atmosphere, to make it funny. I'd rather die than do something like *MasterChef*, which feels a lot more serious. It's that lightness that gives *Bake Off* its big charm,' says Ian Cumming, who appeared in series six. Beca Lyne-Pirkis of series four describes it as 'like having your two naughty best friends with you'. 'Mary and Paul didn't really mix with us, but Mel and Sue did,' recalls Johnny Shepherd. 'That kind of reassured us and made us pleased to be there. They were responsible for a lot of the warmth in the tent that people talk about.'

Mary is of the stiff-upper-lip school: the one thing she frowned upon in the show (apart from Enwezor Nzegwu's shop-bought fondant icing in series five) was blubbing bakers. 'In life, you shouldn't keep bursting into tears. There are occasions when you want to cry your heart out, but not on a television programme. If you do something that doesn't work out, you have to gather yourself up and keep going,' she once said. Mel and Sue disagreed and showed that the presenters have a different role: when tears start to flow, their job is to be there with a kind word and a hug.

When Frances Quinn saw her biscuit tower collapse in a heap in series four, Mel counselled: 'Hold it together, my love,' and then literally held it together for her, standing with her finger on the remaining biscuits to prevent them from hitting the floor. And, of course, one of their other prime functions was to make fun of Paul.

The process for hiring the presenters was exactly the same when the show moved to Channel 4. Love had Prue Leith on board before they booked Noel and Sandi – and with the new foursome ensconced in the tent, the feeling within the production company is that they represent all parts of the audience and there is something for everyone.

*

Nice pear? Perfect nuts? Fancy a lovely tart?

You could argue that Paul and Mary started it with their soggy bottoms, but Mel and Sue's innuendo soon became an integral part of *Bake Off.* By series five – when Sue memorably instructed the bakers that they had 'two hours to pop Mary's cherry. . . in the oven and bring it out again' – the show's social media team was celebrating the duo's Carry On-style wordplay with a #GBBOinnuendo hashtag on Twitter.

Unfortunately, it was all too much for some viewers. Several people complained to BBC *Points of View* that the 'constant smutty remarks' were ruining the show. 'Please ask them to stop spoiling an otherwise delightful programme,' wrote Barbara and Robin Phelps. 'They get smuttier and smuttier, and it is totally unnecessary. Mary Berry looked quite embarrassed on the first programme of this series, and so were we as a family,' said Shirley Fooks (yes, that is a real name). Jean Harris was similarly appalled by Jo Brand's *An Extra Slice*: it was 'controversial, lewd, mucky'. So if you are offended by very bad baking-related puns with a hint of sauce, look away now.

MEL AND SUE'S BEST INNUENDOS:

'Stop touching your dough balls.'

*

'Stand away from your hot baps.'

*

'Stop fiddling with your pirates.'
(To Richard Burr, in series five, as he
perfected his showstopper.)

*

'Keep your biscuits erect!'

*

'Right, bakers. Time to reveal your cracks.'
(Sue on madeira cakes, which should have a
perfect crack down the middle.)

*

'Wow, to be commended on your nuts by
Mary Berry. . .'

*

'Do you need a pair of warm hands – either
on your bag, or on you?' (Mel to Rav Bansal,
in series seven, as he tried to warm up his
biscuit mix.)

*

'Fifteen minutes 'til you give Paul the horn.'

*

'I've never eaten a nun before.' (Sue, on the
'religieuse' technical bake.)

*

'I can't wait to romp in your forest, Iain.'
(Mel, at the news Iain Watters, in series five,
was making a Black Forest gateau.)

By series five, Mary had got in on the act too. 'Some of them have had a good forking,' she said of one baker's biscuits, and on whisking: 'It's all in the wrist action.' And when the innuendo is flying thick and fast, even the most innocent remarks can take on a smutty air. 'I like the flavour of a Cox' is just a comment about an apple, OK? 'My bottom's cracking' is a statement of fact about the underside of a bake, all right? Honestly. What filthy minds you people have.

By the end of the run, even the bakers were doing it. 'Do you need a hand?' Mel asked Candice Brown in series seven as she brought her gingerbread bake up to the judging table. 'Yeah,' Candice replied with a straight face, 'Can you come and grab my jugs?'

*

And so the foursome Sue describes as 'the most ridiculous and over-scrutinized family since the Kardashians' was created. Mary – affectionately known to the other three as 'Bezza' – was the mum, ironing Paul's shirts in her hotel room the night before filming (yes, she really has done that) and telling him off for driving his motorbike too fast. Paul was the dutiful son. Mel and Sue were the wayward cousins who come over on Christmas Day and wreak havoc by eating all the pigs in blankets, acting out rude charades and dressing the dog up as one of Santa's elves. They once stole the keys to Paul's prized Aston Martin during a lull in filming, only to drive it into a ditch. 'Paul had the most spectacular humour failure I've ever seen. . .' said Sue. Mind you, that probably wasn't as bad as the time Mary signed her name on his car with a Sharpie as a joke, not realizing it was a permanent marker. She was last sighted trying to clean it off with a wet wipe. Word has it that Sandi Toksvig, influenced by her new friendship with Paul, is interested in buying a Ford Mustang. . .

3

THE
BAKERS

So how do you go about getting a place on *The Great British Bake Off*? There is only one rule: you have to be an exceptional baker. When the show first started, the producers began to find the talent in obvious ways, mainly application forms. But as the show progressed they also started to look for talent through baking societies and by scouring food-related events and institutions. And they relied on friends and family entering loved ones. Marie Campbell was secretly entered for series six by her daughter. When a show researcher contacted her, Marie thought it was her son playing a practical joke – and hung up. 'When I spoke to my daughter I said, "You'll never believe what your brother's up to now", and she said, "Mum, he was *The Bake Off*!".' Anyway, the very nice young man phoned me back again and it became a wee bit of a joke with us: "Don't hang up!"'

Others took the plunge and applied themselves, without believing they'd ever really get through.

'We went out for Christmas drinks, a group of us from work, and we were making New Year's resolutions. Somebody said they wanted to go to China, somebody else was going to learn tap dancing, and so on. And I said, "I'm definitely going to apply for *Bake Off* this year." So I did. It's a bit like a job application. You think, should I be absolutely honest or embroider a bit? And I went for the honest option.' (Howard Middleton, series 4)

'I first applied the year before I got on. One evening I started to tap away at filling in the form and I just chatted, really. You just speak from the heart – I think you have to on *Bake Off*.

You do expose a lot of who you are. I had a few phone calls, and that was it, I didn't get on. But I had the bit between my teeth then and thought, right, what is it I'm missing? And I think it was a portfolio of pictures, because when you bake for family at home you never really think to take a photograph of every pie you take out of the oven; you're so busy getting it to the table. So the second time around I had a lot more to show.' (Sandy Docherty, series 6)

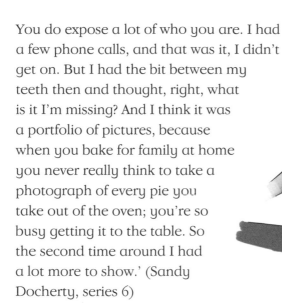

The casting team read each and every application before selecting a few hundred hopefuls for auditions. They are looking for the perfect mix of bakers – both in terms of personality and skill. The contestants are required to bake four times during the selection process – tough going for the production team, for whom eating cake for a living isn't always the dream job: 'For me, casting for *Bake Off* is a little bit like being at a really repetitive drinks party without any cocktails,' says one, who recalls going into a 'sugar-induced trance' after being presented with 120 bakes in a single day.

Not all the bakes get eaten, though. In the auditions for series seven, Louise Williams made an extravagant three-tiered celebration cake with a layer of chocolate and kirsch, another of ginger and sherry, and a bottom layer flavoured with Coca Cola, complete with an intricate chocolate collar. She told the producers that it was really intended to be the centrepiece for her mum's party later that day, so the team kindly took a small slice from the back and left the front untouched.

Hopefuls are asked to bake two things of their choosing at home and bring them to a regional audition. Not too much of a problem if you live nearby, but a logistical challenge if you don't. Judicious use of clingfilm is needed and you might get some odd looks on public transport.

'I made an enormous cake shaped as a fish, with macaron shells as the scales. It was on a board about 60cm x 60cm. I took it up on the train – it was one of the most stressful things I've ever done, to transport it from Portsmouth. I had a date and walnut loaf in a backpack. I got into a black cab at the other end and said, "Please drive slowly. Take as long as you want."' (Enwezor Nzegwu, series 5)

So what do the casting team look for in the selection process?

'The ability to bake is obviously the number one requirement. We have a whole host of brilliant people apply, but unfortunately if you've never tried making bread then the *Bake Off* tent isn't the place for you to learn how to do it,' says one team member.

But producers also take note of the bakers' commitment at an early stage. The second audition of Selasi Gbormittah (series 7) took place over the weekend of his thirtieth birthday celebrations in Prague. He ended up leaving his friends to party on without him as he returned to London to prepare. When asked how he achieved such a perfect crust on his bread, he explained that he had been running late – Selasi is not a man who feels the need to rush – and didn't have time to let it cool. His solution: stick it in a plastic bag and hang it over the handlebars of his motorbike as he rode to the audition.

The bread audition is a tricky one. Manisha Parmar from series three 'must have made the bread at least eleven times that day. It was a really cold day and you have to get the temperature right to prove dough, so I ended up putting it in my bedroom because it was warmer than the kitchen.'

The early auditions are an old-fashioned taste test. Every baker remembers seeing hopefuls arrive with spectacular-looking bakes (we can safely include Enwezor's giant fish cake here) but not making it through to the next round.

'I did these little toffee fruit and nut tarts in a picnic basket and it looked cool. I felt pretty confident. But there were some people who brought some amazing stuff and they didn't make it through so I was definitely immediately aware it was about a little bit more than things just looking amazing.' (Stu Henshall, series 6).

'There were people there of all shape and sizes. I arrived with my meagre offerings. There was a little man who brought the most enormous polenta cake you'd ever seen. There was a woman with her husband in tow, carrying all the stuff, who I thought

must get on because she had made her own marshmallows. But I didn't see her again either.' (Janet Basu, series 2)

The bakers who have impressed are then filmed – this is partly for the programme-makers to have a visual record of the bakers they're considering for the show, and partly to check that the bakers don't clam up on camera as soon as they know they're being recorded. An ability to laugh at yourself in the face of baking disaster is a bonus.

'I made a chocolate cake. I like modelling, so I made a little Mary and a little Paul to go on the cake. And as I went through to see the casting director, Mary's head fell off. I quickly plonked it back on again. There were some very nervous people there, so it was quite nice to provide some light entertainment!' (Marie Campbell, series 6)

'It was a pivotal question for me when they asked, "What do you think you can bring to *Bake Off* that's different?" And I said, "Well, you know, I'm quite creative and energetic. . . And also I really want to see Paul and Mary eat a roadkill pie on television." And [the producer] said, "Oh, nobody has said that before!"' (Ian Cumming, series 6)

'They ushered me into another room and pointed a camera at me. If you've never done it before, even to a handheld camera, it's quite intimidating, them saying, "We're going to see how you look and sound." But we had a good chinwag and a lark. It was great. I walked out with my wife and thought, if nothing else comes of it than this, it was a fun thing to do on a Sunday.' (Richard Burr, series 5)

The successful candidates are then put through their paces by being asked to bake again, this time with the cameras rolling. In the words of one series producer: 'We need to check they can talk and bake at the same time.'

In the early series, Paul and Mary were part of the audition process and judged the bakes just as they do on the show. It gave the prospective bakers a taste of what was to come as Paul deployed his trademark bluntness from the start.

'There was a woman there who had made croissants. She came out of the interview and she threw the croissants in the bin.
I said, "Why did you do that?" And she said, "Paul Hollywood said they weren't good enough because I didn't use the right butter." I thought they looked perfect.' (Lea Harris, series 1)

'We had to bring in pastéis de nata, the little Portuguese tarts. Paul could see I was a bit disgruntled, and asked why I wasn't happy with them. I said it was because they weren't black on top. He said, "Well, they're not supposed to be black on top." I said, "But every one I've ever had has been black on top." "No, they're not supposed to be." I said:

"Yeah, but I wanted them to be." And as I was talking back to him, I could see out of the corner of my eye one of the producers smiling. She came up to me afterwards and said no one had ever talked back to Paul before, and it was great.' (Rob Billington, series 2)

*

Those little vignettes filmed at home – walking the dog, washing up, sitting around the kitchen table with the kids – are the result of a day's filming in which a crew follows the bakers around. As everyone is sworn to secrecy before the show starts that can be a tricky one to explain to the neighbours. Jordan Cox from series five told anyone who asked that the crew were filming a piece on his vintage Chopper bike; Diana Beard's neighbours believed she was selling her house and the estate agent was doing a video tour.

'I don't think any of the neighbours quite knew what they were here for. We were laughing because I do sports massages, so sometimes there's a bit of toing and froing from my house anyway, and I said, "Oh, blimey, they'll think I'm a madam running a suburban brothel like Cynthia Payne!"' (Sandy Docherty, series 6)

*

The final step in the process is a visit to a psychologist. At the beginning, no one had any idea about the level of exposure that being on the show would bring, but as each series went by, the media attention increased.

A programme source points out: 'At this point, and throughout the whole process, it is all about looking after the bakers, about trying to help them imagine what being on the show will be like in every way: the intensity of taking part, the filming process, the scrutiny that comes with being on national television. The duty of care is paramount and an initial psych test is part of that process.'

One of Love's team explains: 'The bakers will have key contacts within the team throughout the process – right from casting through to transmission. We do sit down with the bakers to prepare them for what to expect from taking part in this show, which is primarily very positive and very exciting, but its popularity does mean that there is more interest and more scrutiny.

'Whilst filming in the tent there aren't any of those concerns. No one knows who the bakers are; it's just them, the judges, the presenters and the crew, the *Bake Off* family. Once the show is on screen, the contestants stick together.

'If one of the bakers is concerned that another is struggling, they will call us. Over the years, bakers have been phenomenal at supporting each other, making the experience fun and enjoying the ride together; when a story came out in the paper relating to one of the bakers, they rallied, put it into perspective and made them laugh.'

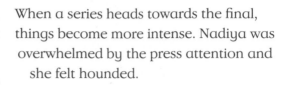

When a series heads towards the final, things become more intense. Nadiya was overwhelmed by the press attention and she felt hounded.

'We did discuss the possibility with Nadiya of moving her family out for a few days,' a source says. In the end, a member of the team moved in with her. 'She felt much calmer knowing someone was on site to advise.'

The psychological assessment may sound overly cautious, but in the year before *Bake Off* began, the welfare of television contestants became a major issue when Susan Boyle was admitted to the Priory clinic after losing the *Britain's Got Talent* final. She had clearly struggled to cope with the pressures of television fame, and the then Culture Secretary, Andy Burnham, warned broadcasters that they must take their duty of care to contestants more seriously.

'I got the impression it was to make sure I could cope with the fact my face would be on television and people would recognize me. I think it's quite a good thing, because it is a bit of a shock having people talk about you as if they know you.' (Rob Billington, series 2)

Finally, the bakers who have passed every test – plus two back-up bakers, in case anyone drops out at the last minute – are informed that they have been chosen to appear on the show.

'Making that call to tell someone that they've made it through to the series is the best part of the job and an absolute delight,' says a member of the team.

And then on a Friday night in May, the bakers meet for the first time in a picturesque corner of England. The next morning, it's time to walk into the tent.

SERIES *1*

THE
BEGINNING

THE CONTESTANTS

Annetha Mills,
30, mother from
Romford, Essex

David Chambers,
31, entrepreneur
from Milton Keynes

Edd Kimber,
24, debt collector
from Bradford

**Jasminder
Randhawa,**
45, credit control
manager from
Birmingham

**Johnny
Shepherd,**
25, research analyst
from St Albans

Lea Harris,
51, retired, from
Midlothian

Louise Brimelow,
44, police officer
from Manchester

Mark Withers,
48, bus driver from
South Wales

Miranda Gore
Browne, 37,
former food buyer,
from Midhurst, West
Sussex

Ruth Clemens,
31, mother-of-three
from Poynton,
Cheshire

Who could have predicted that *Bake Off* would be the biggest TV hit of the decade? Not the critics. Nobody likes to look silly, which is why it's unfortunate that their original verdicts on *Bake Off* were committed to print for us all to read.

The *Daily Mail* introduced it as 'a new series that has a definite whiff of daytime TV about it'. *The Guardian* was pretty sure a programme about baking didn't hold much televisual appeal: 'Once you've seen one person cream butter and sugar together, you have very much seen them all.' *The Daily Telegraph* was merciless, declaring *Bake Off* 'stale, gooey and sickly-sweet. . . a budget *X Factor* for diabetics' and concluding that the whole premise of the show was rubbish: 'As if anyone really cares which amateur baker is slightly less bad than the other.' Yup, it only reached 16 million viewers in the most recent final.

Some got it, though. In the *Express*, Virginia Blackburn praised *Bake Off*'s 'quintessential British charm'. And Andrew Billen of *The Times* wrote that there was 'something so touchingly innocent and vulnerable about the contestants in this cookery competition that it repelled cynicism.'

The ten bakers had been found via adverts placed in magazines and online. Johnny Shepherd stumbled across it when he went on the 'Be on a Show' section of the BBC website to apply for a place in the audience of *Question Time*: 'I was just scrolling down and they had a list of all these different shows, and one of them was something about baking.' Lea Harris was on the same site because her son wanted to appear on the gameshow *Total Wipeout*. 'I got the details and thought, oh, I wonder what else is on here? So I scrolled down and there, in what appeared to me to be huge, nine foot, neon lights, it said: "Are you an amateur baker?" Yes!'

The characters were quickly cast and, before long, the chosen ten were assembled at the Love Production offices in central London, herded onto a minibus and driven to a hotel in the Cotswolds. It felt a bit like a school trip. None of the contestants had a clue what they were in for.

Watch series one now and it has a charming feel about it, decidedly less slick than in later years. Production crew can be seen wandering around in the back of shots. Cardboard boxes are piled up beside the fridge. At the beginning of one episode, Mel and Sue did their link to camera near a dilapidated caravan. Just out of view: a ceiling area filled with balloons by the sound technicians to muffle the echoes. As more than one contestant put it: 'They often seemed to be making it up as they went along.' The bakers had been told so little about what to expect that they had no idea the show was to be filmed in a tent. When the mini-bus pitched up at the location on the first morning, they thought they'd stumbled upon a village fête.

The judges and presenters quickly found their footing, though. Mel and Sue – who described themselves as 'the cheeky bookends' to the main act of judging – larked about and provided the bakers with a shoulder to cry on, doling out hugs to the exiting baker in what they liked to call a 'Mel and Sue sandwich'. Mary and Paul had their good cop/bad cop act, with Paul fixing those Arctic blue eyes on a nervous baker and saying something disparaging, then Mary throwing in an encouraging smile and trying to find something, anything, positive to say (while always rhyming 'layers' with 'pears').

The foundations of the show were laid in series one: the signature bake, in which the bakers follow a recipe of their own choosing while putting their own twist on it; the technical challenge, which requires the bakers to create something complicated with no forewarning, against the clock and following minimal instructions; and the fancy-pants final bake, not yet known as 'the showstopper' because nobody had dreamed up the name. The jaunty music was there, and the cream Smeg fridges and Union Jack bunting. But some things didn't work, and were tweaked for series two:

THE VOICEOVER.

A narration by actor Steven Noonan was replaced by the voices of Mel and Sue themselves in later series.

THE HISTORY BITS.

Because the show was originally commissioned by the BBC's documentary department, it was heavy on the history. At one stage, people were hired to dress in period costume and come into the tent, footage which ended up on the cutting room floor. There were originally three separate historical bits (later reduced to one, a bonus for Paul, who admitted he 'always fast-forwards through that bit'), which included Sue pootling off in a sensible hatchback to find out the history of cakes, or Mel donning a red nylon hairnet to tour a McVitie's factory. It's like that bit on *Escape to the Country* where the couple just want to see how many bathrooms they can get for their £800,000, but instead have to smile politely through a demonstration of pencil-making. They did a game job, but Mel later admitted: 'I don't remember a single gag getting through series one.'

THE TOURING TENT.

Originally, the programme moved around the country each week, according to the theme of the episode. So it was pasties in Cornwall, puddings in Bakewell, scones in Scotland's Scone Palace, bread near a windmill in Kent. The series kicked off in Kingham in the Cotswolds, chosen because it had once been named Britain's favourite village.

*

Bake Off without the tent just wouldn't be *Bake Off*. With the show changing location each episode, a studio was out of the question. The tent had the added benefits of being quick to put up and take down – during that first year, the crew became so efficient that they could pack up the whole thing

in three hours. And the look was perfect for the show, as art director Dom Clasby explains: 'It has that idyllic sense of Englishness – the greenery, the outdoors, the fact it all stayed in a tent come wind or rain. It reflects those slightly barmy English ways.'

The set designer was James Zafar, who had also created the look for *MasterChef* and worked on *The Big Breakfast* and *TFI Friday*. He worked closely with the team to bring the set to life.

James brought fun and warmth and a quirky sense of Englishness to the design, stringing the tent with Union Jack bunting. 'He didn't want it to look like a professional kitchen but something more domestic, more homely, as it is an amateur competition. The colours had to be nothing too jumpy-out; it was when Farrow & Ball was really coming onto the scene. And one of the key design elements that stood out on that set was the sunburst right at the back. That was James's crowning glory,' says Dom. 'He was a fabulous chap, really talented and an absolute stickler for detail. He was old school.'

James died from cancer in 2016, aged 48, and his name in the credits is a record of his crucial role in *Bake Off*'s success.

It was Dom's job to pull James's vision together. 'The set designer comes up with the overall look and design, and the art director helps facilitate that – sourcing props, choosing colour palettes, overseeing the build and watching it come to life.'

With the help of a buyer, the tent was kitted out with retro-looking goods: Smeg fridges and KitchenAid mixers. Both ended up proving controversial. After one viewer complained to the *Radio Times* that he had stopped counting after seeing the Smeg logo thirty-seven times in one episode, the BBC was found to have breached product placement guidelines. And when the programme-makers decided to substitute the mixers with an alternative from Kenwood in series six, viewers were dismayed. (Sample Twitter comment: "When did GBBO move away from the beautiful vintage KitchenAid mixers to those postmodern monstrosities?!".)

And if things don't look exactly as they're supposed to when you arrive on a set – well, you can always improvise. As Dom recalls: 'I remember on the first show, someone saying, "Where's the big tree we're meant to have in the corner?" It hadn't made it onto the truck. One of my carpenters, who was very resourceful, went away and came back about twenty minutes later with half a tree. I didn't ask where from. . .'

*

There were a number of problems with the touring tent set-up. First, because the tent didn't have a permanent home, facilities were lacking. If you'd found yourself in Kingham that first weekend of filming, you might have spotted Mary Berry queuing for a public loo. At least that was nearby in the village hall. 'When we filmed in Mousehole [in Cornwall] we had to use the loos on the quay,' remembers Miranda Gore Browne. 'In the middle of filming, we'd have to walk out through the crowds, go down to the quayside, and queue up. There wasn't a mirror, only one of those metal sheet mirrors they have to combat vandalism, so Ruth and I had to do our make-up in the wing mirror of a Land Rover Discovery. How would Candice have coped with that?!'

Because the tent was pitched in the middle of towns and villages, curious members of the public could wander over and have a nosy. The little white picket fence that runs around the tent was an attempt to keep people from poking their heads in, but it didn't put everybody off. Miranda says: 'People would yell, "Time's up!" "You need to stop now!" "Ooh, you're going to take it out looking like that, are you?".'

Carting everything up and down the country was a monumental task for the crew, who encountered different challenges at every turn. 'We had an articulated lorry and a Luton van. One of the location managers misunderstood when we first set up and hadn't realized that we couldn't drive the lorry onto the green of Britain's favourite village, so we had to get some muscle in. Each of the guys from the crewing company had to carry 35 kg for over a kilometre.' With no running water, 'we were lugging 25-litre jerry cans of water across a car park every 20 minutes to empty grey water and refill them.' But Dom remembers it fondly. 'It was a good bunch of people working crazy hours and pulling off something that hadn't really been done before.'

The logistics of moving to a different location each week also took its toll on the bakers, who had jobs and children and lives to juggle, never mind travel to opposite ends of the country. But, more than anything, it was expensive. When the producers sat down with the BBC to plan series two, Love boss Richard McKerrow argued in favour of the touring tent because he believed audiences enjoyed seeing different areas of the country. But budget requirements meant a permanent location was essential. And it would help if the location was somewhere secluded and away from traffic – the country-idyll feel was slightly marred by glimpses of cars through the tent's PVC windows.

There is one small contributor to *Bake Off*'s success: a constant refining of the format. As each series went by, things that didn't work were quietly shelved. The production got slicker, the catchphrases got better, Mary's hair got bigger. The first series felt like an experiment in finding the perfect mix.

Series one also saw the first use of a phrase that would become very, very familiar. 'The last thing you want to do,' said Paul as he discussed baking the perfect pie, 'is cut through that crispy top, hit that beautiful inside and then hit a really soggy bottom.'

BAKE OFF TERMS

Under-baked/over-baked:
Paul's favourite insult.

*

Even bake: not the above.

*

A good crumb: crumb that is not too dense,
not too crumby.

*

Nice snap: what your biscuits and bread
sticks should have.

*

Rough puff: a supposedly simple-to-make
form of puff pastry.

*

Crème pât: to show you are an expert in
these things, you must never refer to this
by its full name of crème pâtissière.
It's essentially a fancy custard.

*

Deconstructed: the sides fell off and you didn't have time to stick them back on.

*

Ganache: a sauce made with chocolate and cream. As in: 'OK, bakers, fifteen minutes until your ganache hits my guh-nashers.' (Thanks, Sue.)

*

Artisan: nobody is quite sure what this means, except that an artisan loaf of bread will look wonky and cost you at least £3. Sandy Docherty from series six has the measure of this one: 'At the second audition we had to take up a white loaf. I adopted the word "artisan" because it seems to excuse a lot of randomness. When you say "artisan" everyone just expects it to be a bit messy. . .'

*

Proving drawer: somewhere you put your dough to warm and rise. Every *Bake Off* workstation has one, but you don't need one, according to James Morton from series three, who went on to write a book about bread: 'Don't buy one, unless you like to warm commercial quantities of plates prior to dinner.'

One man who would be intrinsic to the show, and who was there from episode one, was the illustrator Tom Hovey. He landed the job almost by accident – after studying for an illustration degree in Bournemouth, he was working in 'a pretty rough pub' in

London to make ends meet. A friend who worked in TV got him a temporary job as a runner helping out in the edit suite where a director and editor were putting together the first series of *Bake Off.* 'They mentioned that there was a visual element missing from the show and they were thinking of including some illustration to help the viewers understand what the bakers were intending to create. I said I could do it, pitched a few ideas and got the gig. A serious bit of serendipity,' he told Cass Art in 2016.

Hovey works from photographs of the bakes (he never sees them in real life), which he sketches in pencil, inks with a pen over a lightbox, then colours in Photoshop. As the bakes have become more elaborate, so the illustrations have got a bit fancier. It takes him a week to illustrate all the bakes from one episode. Last year he brought out his own *Bake Off* colouring book.

The music is also a big part of the *Bake Off* viewing experience. Tom Howe is the composer. His varied CV includes Disney's *Monkey Kingdom*, the Channel 4 documentary *The Liquid Bomb Plot* and the *Wonder Woman* film.

'I was sent some clips from the show,' the composer recalls. 'Although now there's probably a lot of stuff that sounds and looks like *Bake Off*, at the time there wasn't. Everything was like *MasterChef*, very serious. I remember watching this video of Mary Berry making a meringue or something and thinking it was really different and really light.

'We decided it should be really fun. That's where I ended up using some Latin rhythms, and it's got timbales in, which are like a Latin percussion instrument, along with strings. But there are no minor chords in it, which is unusual for TV. If you think of *Hell's Kitchen* or *MasterChef* or *The Apprentice*, all those shows are in a minor key and have a lot of gravitas. And *Bake Off* is in a

major key. It's quite hard to write in major key and not make it sound really cheesy, so that was the challenge.

'Bits of it sound very English, I hope – the harmonies are quite classical. I was listening to so many different things to try and get some ideas, and one of them was Elgar. Not that it particularly sounds like Elgar, the arrangement isn't similar, but some of the chord choices are similar. If you think of something like *Nimrod*, that's in major key. It's got a kind of Englishness about it.'

Howe has fielded offers for the music to be used on adverts, but all have been turned down. The theme has remained unique to *Bake Off*. He has also resisted any urge to tinker with the theme. 'And that's quite unusual, because if you look at news themes or something long-running like *The One Show*, the music is updated. But the *Bake Off* music fundamentally hasn't changed.

'It's probably my most recognizable piece of music, and it was totally unexpected. I spend a lot of time in Los Angeles these days because I'm working on films; I go for a meeting and they want to talk about *Bake Off*. It's never happened with anything else I've done. But it's just loved by everybody.'

*

Lea Harris, a jolly retiree from Scotland, was the first baker to be sent home in the very first episode of *Bake Off*, after a crazy showstopper involving a whole pineapple protruding from a chocolate cake – a creation she now refers to as 'the psycho pineapple cake'. ('One of my friends said, "You need height on a cake." Hence that bloody pineapple.') But she had a ball. 'It was just such fun,' she says. 'Yes, it was very stressful. You go back into the tent on that Sunday morning filled with trepidation. But the camaraderie was fantastic.'

Her first bake was a cranberry and pistachio cake, and there were several things wrong with it. 'It didn't help that when I took it out of the oven I dropped it. You didn't see the reason on the show, but it was because I'd singed my oven gloves and when I looked down they were almost on fire, so my immediate reaction was to pull my hands apart. I was just really relieved by the fact I didn't swear!'

She became fast friends with fellow baker Louise Brimelow. 'While we were waiting for Paul and Mary to come round and judge the cakes, Louise was behind me. I just lent up against Louise's workstation and I said, "I hate that cake. I just hate it." And she said, "Lea, have you got good kids?" I said yes. "Got enough money to pay the bills?" Yes. "Got a good husband?" Yes. And she said: "It's only a f***ing cake." And that became our in-joke. Whenever I see Louise now and I moan about something, she says, "Lea! It's only a f***ing cake."' The key to enjoying your *Bake Off* experience, according to many of the bakers, is not to take it too seriously.

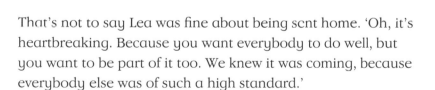

That's not to say Lea was fine about being sent home. 'Oh, it's heartbreaking. Because you want everybody to do well, but you want to be part of it too. We knew it was coming, because everybody else was of such a high standard.'

The tone of the show was set in the first episode, when Mark Withers, a bus driver from the Welsh Valleys, broke down in tears when his signature marmalade cake sank in the middle. Here was a grown man crying on TV in a cake competition, but the viewers' instinct wasn't to mock – instead we wanted to give him a cuddle. Which is exactly what Sue did, gently chiding him to wipe away those tears or he'd end up with a salt water cake for his next challenge. Everything we came to love about *Bake Off* was encapsulated in that scene. And when Mark was also knocked out of the competition at the end of the episode, we felt sad, even though we'd only spent an hour in his company.

Mark was diagnosed with cancer two years after he appeared on the show. 'The doctor told him he had one or two years left, but in the end he had nine months,' says his widow, Elaine. 'He had a little pension, and we decided to spend some of the money on things he really wanted to do. We went to see a show in London, and stayed in a swanky hotel. And we went to a reunion of the bakers at a cake show in Birmingham. Mark was very ill and we had to get him a scooter because he couldn't walk. But he made it there. He wanted to see everybody one more time. I remember seeing Mary Berry and Paul Hollywood, and Paul said, "Keep fighting".'

Sadly, Mark died soon afterwards, in May 2013, aged fifty-one. Elaine has kept a scrapbook, a sort of 'This Is Your Life' for her husband of nearly 30 years, and in amongst the treasured family photographs are a letter of condolence from Mary, the contract he signed to appear on *Bake Off* and pictures of him on set with Mel and Sue. 'He was so excited about being on the show. When he came back from that weekend I asked how he'd got on and he said, "I'm not through to next time, but I still enjoyed it." He was chuffed that his Victoria sandwich did quite well. And that moment when he cried over his cake – well, he's quite emotional, our Mark. It wasn't out of character. If anything, he got even more enthused about baking after being on the show. He was always taking cakes in for everyone at the bus company. Even when he was ill, he made cupcakes for the Macmillan nurses.'

*

The contestants – only ten for this first series – were a diverse bunch. There was Annetha Mills, a mother from Essex, who wanted her cakes to fuse British and West Indian culture; Johnny Shepherd, a nicely spoken young man from St Albans, who had just quit his job as a research analyst and wanted to re-open his grandfather's bakery; Jas Randhawa, a credit control manager from Sutton Coldfield, who tested out her bakes on colleagues; laidback Ruth Clemens from Cheshire, who managed to finish each challenge with acres of time to spare; busy mum Miranda Gore Browne from West Sussex; Louise Brimelow, a straight-talking police officer from Greater Manchester and David Chambers, a shaven-headed entrepreneur from Milton Keynes, who the producers marked out as having perfectionist tendencies.

And there was Edd Kimber, a bespectacled litigation clerk in the debt-collection department at Yorkshire Bank. 'Baking's my obsession. It's what I think about all the time,' he said the first time viewers were introduced to him. 'It's my hobby, it's my love, it's everything to me, really. I adore it.'

Mel and Sue developed a neat way of protecting the bakers: if an over-eager crew member thrust a camera into the face of an emotional baker, the presenters would dash over and swear loudly – ensuring the footage could never be broadcast. 'I think they were the perfect combination and a lovely balance. Sue is kind of like the older sister who loves you really, whereas Mel is much more maternal. Mel would be like, "Are you all right, darling?" What we felt was that they were saying, "We really care about you guys, we're on your side,"' says Kimberley Wilson, finalist in series four. 'Mel and Sue are terribly naughty, but because they make you laugh it relaxes you. I think they are two of the nicest people on the planet,' says another series four alumna, Christine Wallace.

Niceness is under-rated. It's not exactly seen as the greatest compliment ('What's her new boyfriend like?' 'Well, you know, he's. . . nice.'). But niceness is *Bake Off*'s calling card, and millions of us are drawn to it. 'It has the age-old thing that shows like this must have: jeopardy. But it also has an extraordinary warmth,' says William Sitwell, food critic, *Waitrose Magazine* editor and regular guest on the slightly less nice *MasterChef*.

'A lot of shows are about jeopardy and real people, things like *X Factor* and *Britain's Got Talent*, and part of the reason we watch them is because they build up these people as freaks and then you relish with an almost evil zeal their complete collapse and humiliation. And bravely, given the appetite for such things, this show doesn't do that. No one enjoys people's failures on *Bake Off*, in fact, they find it very sad and get quite emotional. And that is partly because of the presenter team. There's just no deliberate meanness and it has succeeded on the back of that, which is actually a lovely thing.'

Ugnė Bubnaityte, who appeared in series six, sums
up the appeal of the show: 'Harmony. There is a
little bit of happiness, a little bit of failure, a little
bit of everything. But it's feel good. There's
no bitching, no shouting, no swearing. Just
talking about soggy bottoms.'

*

The grand final, in London, featured
three bakers: Edd, Ruth and Miranda.
Families and former contestants gathered
for the garden party that was to become
a feature of every series. Miranda's lemon
cupcakes failed to excite Paul (not your fault, Miranda – Paul is
so unenthusiastic about cupcakes that by 2016 he was declaring
that if presented with another one, 'I'd ram it into someone's
face, honestly I would'). It became a two-horse race between
Ruth and Edd. Ruth was displaying her trademark cool – 'cooler
than a refrigeration unit in the Arctic,' as Sue had it – yet told
how the competition had given her confidence for the first time

in years, after waving her friends off to university while she was a stay-at-home mum. 'Paul said my lemon cake could be served to the Queen. Served to the Queen!' she said, bursting with pride. Edd was, by his own account, a bundle of stress. But he had the edge, and his caramel and banana mini-cakes won the day. Mel cried, Sue cried, Edd cried, Paul offered him a manly handshake and a mini-FA Cup trophy trimmed with ribbons (the *Bake Off* cake stand was yet to come).

*

The final attracted 2.75 million viewers, a good audience for BBC2 and enough to earn a recommission for a second series. 'I think baking's making a bit of a comeback, actually,' Mel mused. Oh, Mel, you have no idea what's coming.

The final episode ended with a postscript: 'Edd quit his job at the bank two days after winning *Bake Off*.' Baking, you see, can change your life.

THE FLAVOURS

The technical bakes are a test of how well you can follow a recipe against the clock. The showstoppers are all about looking spectacular. But the signature bakes are the surprises you don't see coming.

Series one was all about introducing viewers to the idea of the signature bake: a classic recipe served with a twist. Hence the first week saw Ruth's twist on a lemon drizzle cake – the addition of fresh cream and home-made lemon curd (Mary: 'It is a far cry from lemon drizzle cake.') – and Jonathan's twist on a carrot cake, which involved adding lime to the cream cheese icing. For Biscuit

Week, the bakers were instructed by Sue to create something that reflected 'your personality in a biscuit'. Miranda did this with style, baking beautiful vanilla biscuits iced to look like shoes, handbags and teapots. Edd doused his oatmeal and raisin cookies in Sauternes. Louise accidentally added seven times the correct amount of sugar to her stained-glass window shortbread. And David produced decidedly unsweet cheddar cheese and rosemary oatcakes.

Jasminder Randhawa saved her wackiest ideas for the showstoppers. One week she decided to add space dust to her meringues, thus creating every eight-year-old's fantasy meal. Continuing the theme in Bread Week, she put Mars Bars in her pain au chocolat and Jelly Tots in her tutti frutti wheels. Dentists across Britain recoiled in horror.

MARY BERRY

Watch the first episodes and Mary looks lovely, of course she does. But as the series went by, Mary transformed. The hair got bigger. The mascara-ed eyelashes grew longer. Granny pastels were out and zingy brights were in. The woman is in her eighties. She looks AMAZING.

Mary became *Bake Off*'s fashion icon – well, until Noel Fielding came along. Girls in their teens began coveting Mary's jackets. A Zara bomber she wore in 2012 promptly sold out and was being offered on eBay for £200 (although, to be fair, things at Zara always sell out. But let's stick with the PR hype and not be cynical), as did an M&S stork print bomber. She looked so chic

you didn't notice that she had a hot water bottle tucked inside her jacket to ward off the cold.

She even made number seventy-four in *GQ*'s list of the world's sexiest women, one place behind Angelina Jolie but several places in front of Jennifer Lopez. Asked about it during a talk at the Oxford Union, Berry was momentarily taken aback: 'I'd no idea! It's a very nice thought.' And one beat later, with a twinkle in her eye: 'But why was I only seventy-fourth?'

Mary gave style writer Liz Jones a tour of her wardrobe after the third series had turned her into a bona fide fashion icon, saying she was 'flabbergasted' by the attention. 'The bomber was a bit of fun, and it was roomy enough to be worn over thermal underwear and several sweaters, as it was always so cold in the marquee,' she explained.

The judges are usually shot from the waist up so it's all about the jackets, whether a hot-pink Ralph Lauren number or a botanical print biker from French Connection.

The look she aimed to achieve was 'summery, positive and encouraging', and her 'secret weapon' is her dressmaker: 'She alters every single thing I buy. Take that Zara bomber: after I wore it on the show, she shortened the sleeves. Long sleeves keep getting mucky, they get covered in flour.' On her bottom half she wears jeans, and manages to make them look smart. 'Bezza loves a jean,' says Mel.

And how did Mary manage to remain so slim while chowing

down on cakes and puddings all weekend long? 'With great difficulty,' is her answer. 'I have been large in my time. I know that if I were really quite big, people would look at me and say, "Well, that's what happens if you eat cake." So I'm fairly disciplined,' she told *Bake Off* fans at the Hay Festival.

'I make myself have one piece of toast at breakfast – I would like three. When I'm doing *Bake Off* I always have soup every day for my lunch because I have plenty of food around that. Every evening we all have supper together and I nearly always have two first courses. I have a lot of salads and things. It's a matter of grasping the nettle and keeping it under control.'

Skip forward to the Channel 4 series and there was a mini-furore when Noel was quoted as saying he wouldn't be tasting the bakes. 'I get more work when I'm thinner, so I can't put on weight,' he said with a straight face. 'I don't eat anything. I'm like a plant.' He later clarified that he'd been joking. Phew.

In that same talk, Mary also revealed she had smartened up Paul's image since the programme began. 'He used to wear these T-shirts with a round neck and short sleeves and I said, "You look much better in shirts," like his mother would. So now he always wears a shirt.'

While Mary has always been impeccably dressed, Paul hails from the Jeremy-Clarkson-dad-jeans school of dressing. When the judges and presenters line up to address the bakers, he stands with hands on hips and feet planted apart. His salt-and-pepper hair perfectly styled, his beard neatly trimmed. And then there are those Paul Newman blue eyes. Alexa Chung, who appeared on a charity edition of the show in 2015, once said: 'You know, when famous people have shiny eyes? Paul's are crystal clear. Celebrity eyes.'

SERIES 2

HEART-
THROBS
AND
SQUIRRELS

THE CONTESTANTS

Ben Frazer,
31, graphic designer
from Northampton

Holly Bell,
31, advertising
executive from
Leicester

Ian Vallance,
40, English Heritage
fundraiser from
Dunstable

Janet Basu,
63, teacher from
Formby, Merseyside

Jason White,
19, student from
Croydon

Joanne Wheatley,
41, housewife from
Ongar, Essex

Keith Batsford,
31, househusband
from Arlesey,
Bedfordshire

**Mary-Anne
Boermans,** 45,
housewife from
Kidderminster,
Worcestershire

Robert Billington,
25, photographer
from London

Simon Blackwell,
31, rugby coach
from Norfolk

Urvashi Roe,
40, head of
marketing from
London

Yasmin Limbert,
43, childminder from
the Wirral

Series two saw the birth of a new phenomenon: the *Bake Off* heart-throb. Rob Billington was a twenty-five-year-old photographer who dreamed of becoming a professional baker in Paris (according to the blurb – now he says he has no idea where the BBC got that from, and he's happily settled in north London). Rob wore a flannel checked shirt and had dimples and hair that flopped into his eyes. He had the air of a man who was hungover from Saturday night but was still willing to go to Sainsbury's Local on Sunday morning to buy ingredients to make you pancakes. He was so adorable that when he tipped his chocolate celebration cake onto the floor in the first episode, about as big a disaster as it's possible to get on *Bake Off*, even Paul pitched in to scrape it off the fuzzy carpet tile and rescue Rob from oblivion.

Twitter was in a collective swoon before he even started his first bake. 'I'm totally in love with Rob,' was a regular refrain. 'He can come and make me a lemon tart any day.' 'Young, fit, bakes cupcakes #perfect.' 'ROB MARRY ME.' *Heat* magazine ran a photoshoot alongside an article crowning him 'TV's Hottest New Bloke'. A 'Rob Billington Can Squeeze My Icing Bag Any Day' page still exists on Facebook. The BBC, spotting a new market of lovestruck Rob fans, cannily chose him as the one baker to appear on the front of that year's *Bake Off* cookbook.

It was all a bit discombobulating for the man himself. He had joined Twitter a few weeks before the series aired and was shocked to find his attractiveness the subject of national debate. The messages started arriving 'literally five minutes into the first episode. I was getting hundreds of tweets every single time. It was insane. Quite a few people said they loved me. Which was really weird.' There was also the occasional detractor. When the series was rerun on a cable channel, someone went to the trouble of setting up a 'Rob Sucks' Twitter account. Which he found hilarious.

From that point on, the unveiling of each year's bakers had fans scanning the line-up for a potential love object. Series three delivered it in the form of James Morton, a medical student from Scotland, with a natty line in Argyll knitwear. But nobody came close to Rob's heart-throb status until series six, and the arrival of Dr Tamal Ray. Many of the nation's women were left disappointed when he told an interviewer mid-way through the series, when asked if there was a girlfriend in his life: 'I wouldn't have a girlfriend, I would have a boyfriend.' The nation's gay men rejoiced. Nadiya's husband, Abdal, also developed a fan following after he was featured in the show ('a stone cold hotty', as one Twitter user put it). And series seven gave us Selasi Gbormittah, the most laidback contestant ever to grace the show. Even Paul Hollywood had a man crush on Selasi.

'I had more of a relationship with Selasi than with anyone else over the last seven years,' he says. 'He's a biker. We swapped numbers, we've promised we'll go out for a bike ride together. I spent more time with Selasi than any other baker.'

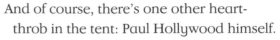

And of course, there's one other heart-throb in the tent: Paul Hollywood himself. When Mary is approached by fans in the street, the question she is asked most is: 'Are Paul's eyes really that blue?' She replies that yes, they really are. He was soon universally referred to as 'the George Clooney of baking'. 'Hot baker Paul Hollywood is making temperatures soar in kitchens all over Britain,' panted *The Mirror*. When he goes on tour or gives cookery demonstrations at food festivals, the atmosphere is more hen party with the Chippendales than sedate WI baking seminar. Paul insists he is embarrassed by the sex symbol tag, describing himself as 'just a normal fat bloke from the north'. Not too embarrassed though – on those tours he walks on stage to a Lenny Kravitz record called 'Strut'.

*

These days, it's easy to judge a contestant's popularity with the viewing nation: just check Twitter. Back in the summer of 2011, the social media platform was not yet mainstream – the technology editor of *The Daily Telegraph* had to write a piece explaining to readers what Twitter actually was, noting that 'users need to remember that the vast majority of people aren't on it.'

But Twitter fell for *Bake Off*. Television executives may talk about the decline of linear viewing (when you sit down to watch a programme as it is live on TV), now that everyone has catch-up and can watch shows at a time to suit them. Long gone are the days when sitcoms such as *Only Fools and Horses* or *To The Manor Born* could attract regular audiences of 20 million an episode. Nowadays you might find mum and dad surfing through hundreds of channels (and complaining that there's still nothing to watch) and the kids flicking through YouTube videos on their mobile phones. Yet the ratings for *Bake Off* demonstrate there is still such a thing as appointment-to-view television. And while that may sound like an old-fashioned concept, it is fuelled by the very modern phenomenon of social media.

Bake Off was a programme that Twitter users watched in real time together. It was a joyful shared experience. And when the people you follow start tweeting about a show, you take a look at it too, to find out what they're on about. Twitter drove the popularity of the show among a young demographic. 'I guess Twitter was different then,' says Rob. 'Now it's more of a normal way of reacting with people; then it was still a bit of a novelty.'

2010 was 'a time when Twitter was really taking off, and a time when broadcasters wanted to create occasions where everybody is sitting down and watching the same thing at the same time, because the rise of catch-up meant nobody was watching anything live any more unless it was a football match,' says Professor Liz Evans, assistant professor in film and television studies at the University of Nottingham, who researches television audiences and their use of technology.

'So *Bake Off* fitted this particular moment. And it helped that it was a well-made programme, and well-cast, with interesting characters that people wanted to talk about. It was hitting a particular moment when those social media platforms were coming out.

'I think a lot of it comes down to the fact that *Bake Off* is a show with nice people on it, doing a nice thing – making cake, which is pretty apolitical, isn't it? – in a nice, friendly atmosphere. It's a safe space, lovely and comforting, which is particularly appealing in the last few years when spaces like Twitter have become more problematic.'

That problematic side did rear its head in series five of *Bake Off*, when speech therapist Claire Goodwin became the target of Twitter trolls. She went out in episode one, after her chocolate cherry mini-cakes failed to make the grade despite a generous sprinkling of gold love hearts. Claire was, by any measure, quite lovely. Yet she was mocked online about her weight. She responded with a brave blog post denouncing the keyboard warriors.

Yet the vast majority of social media comments about *Bake Off* are positive, and that has a trickle-down effect. As Professor Evans explains: 'Of course there are plenty of viewers who don't use Twitter. But the online buzz gets picked up everywhere and gains momentum beyond social media. So even if you're not tweeting yourself, it feeds your perception of the programme and the sense that everyone is watching it, and then you see the headlines and the fact it's becoming so highly rated and it just builds.'

The stats show how big *Bake Off* has been on Twitter. There were 120,000 tweets about Bingate, not to mention a #justiceforiain hashtag, from series five. That year's final attracted 135,000 tweets; the following year, there were almost 250,000 tweets about Nadiya's emotional win. The most tweeted-about television star in the autumn of 2016 wasn't Jeremy Clarkson, heading back to our screens in the massively hyped successor to *Top Gear*, but *Bake Off*'s Candice Brown (series 7).

'The people on *Bake Off* are being themselves in what seems to be quite an unvarnished way, and people respond to that,' says Alice Beverton Palmer, media partnerships manager at Twitter (and also a massive *Bake Off* fan). 'One of the striking things for me every year has been how wonderfully diverse the contestants are. There are older women, amazing women who have been looking after their families and are finally doing something for themselves, people of colour, gay people. I think people respond to that, especially on Twitter.

'And in the same way Mel and Sue are protective of the bakers in the tent, so there is a huge, positive community being similarly protective on Twitter.'

Viewers watching alone at home can enter into a conversation about the show as they watch it. 'It's so instant you don't feel like you're on your own because everyone who's interested in the same thing is there in your phone at that moment. With Bingate, it was one of those moments that Twitter is so good for, where you're going: "Are we all seeing the same thing? Oh my God!"'

The rise of *Bake Off* coincided with a new kid on the media block: Buzzfeed. There was a time not so long ago when the company was treated as a bit of a joke by the traditional print press, but it wasn't long before every newspaper was aping its format. In 2013, the company opened its UK office; by the end of that year it was reporting more than ten million users a month. News consumption was changing, as people increasingly looked at content on mobile phones.

Buzzfeed's light-hearted tone and its format of listicles, gifs and memes was perfectly suited to *Bake Off*. And if you have no idea what that sentence means, you're over the age of thirty. Here's a few sample Buzzfeed headlines, so you get the idea:

The Pencil Behind Richard's Ear Should Be Your Favourite Contestant On *The Great British Bake Off* [including pictures of every time Richard (series 5) had a pencil behind his ear. It was nine times]

21 Of The Best Panicked Faces On *Bake Off* Of All Time

69 Thoughts I Had Watching The First New Episode Of *The Great British Bake Off*

31 Pictures of Selasi From *Bake Off* That Might Make You Pregnant

Meet The Sick Cat Who Got Better By Watching The GBBO [his name was Roger]

(Incidentally, you will seldom find a '10 things. . .' list on Buzzfeed, or any other website, these days because data has shown that people are more likely to click on online lists if they have an odd number in the title.)

During series seven alone, Buzzfeed's UK site published seventy-four *Bake Off* articles. It's safe to say Scott Bryan, the site's entertainment editor, is a *Bake Off* fan – so much of a *Bake Off* fan that, in the name of journalism, he baked every technical bake in series six and seven. His first piece was titled 'I Baked

Every Technical Challenge From *The Great British Bake Off* And It Was A F***ing Disaster'.

'*Bake Off* is absolutely mad with younger viewers. Our readers primarily go from the age of fifteen or sixteen right into their twenties and thirties, and I reckon that's exactly the core audience of *Bake Off*,' he says. But why do young people love it so much? 'For many years, channels have been trying to put young people in a box, to try and think what they would like and then dumb it down. The thing about *Bake Off* is: it's probably become popular with young people because it has never tried to cater for them. So many shows you see are patronizing and lowbrow, because they think that's what young people will be interested in. But *Bake Off* isn't trying to be cool in any way.'

The show is perfect for social media, he says. 'The interaction that we see on people's feeds and on Tumblr is the same level you'd get for something like The Eurovision Song Contest, making jokes or talking about certain people they love. It's partly because they have such a wide variety of bakers.' While some of their most popular posts were about Tamal (series 6), 'because he was young and he was hot and he was single', Scott's favourite recent contestant was sixty-six-year-old Val Stones (series 7) from Somerset, 'because she had such a great outlook on life. No matter what feedback she got, she always ignored it.'

Scott's idea of attempting every technical bake came about sort of by accident. He planned a one-off, with a colleague filming his efforts, making a frosted walnut cake from series six. 'It wasn't that bad, apart from I didn't have any cutlery or anything so I couldn't mix the ingredients together. And then I thought, I'm just going to keep going. I was just doing it with my partner filming me, in our house, and it wasn't meant for a Buzzfeed article. But I'd take the bakes in for my colleagues to taste, and after four or five weeks my boss said, "So when's the article coming out?".' Scott would watch the episode on Wednesday, buy the ingredients on Thursday, then start baking after dinner that night. 'Sometimes I would finish dinner and think, oh, this'll take an hour, an hour-and-a-half. And we were still doing it 'til 2.30 in the morning. I lost my frickin' mind. It didn't harm my relationship but it definitely tested it. . .' It was worth it, though. The resulting article was read by 1.3 million people.

But while millennials and Twitter users were mining *Bake Off* for comedy and helping to turn it into a national talking point, they weren't the only people watching it. *Bake Off* has cross-generational appeal, a programme that young and old can watch together.

Shows that can be watched by the entire family are gold dust to broadcasters. Soaps are no-go areas. *Doctor Who* is too dark for young children. *Strictly Come Dancing* skews towards a female audience, and anything narrated by Sir David Attenborough inevitably features cute animals meeting a gory end. But, as Mary said when she appeared at the Oxford Union: 'We have kept it as a family show. There's so much swearing, so much hype, in every [other] programme. In our programme, I'm teaching all the way through and I'm thinking of the family that are watching. We have the biggest viewership on television and it's all the family: it's nan, it's the father or partner who has given up his football because the rest of the lot want to watch it, it's the baby on the knee – and when they've watched it they want to go and do it. It's a happy programme.'

And as if the gorgeous bakes, Mel and Sue's gags, and Rob's dimples weren't enough to get people talking, there was also the squirrel.

The programme's editor regularly cuts away to shots outside the tent: sweeping shots of the parkland, sheep munching grass, raindrops on a leaf, that sort of thing. The owner of one of the location venues, Linda Hill, recalls the hours put into getting those shots: 'They bring in a drone on the last day and take it up over everything. But for the close-ups, the director used to arrive very, very early in the morning and you'd find him lying for hours in the grass trying to get a caterpillar or something.'

The final of series two featured a squirrel which – how can we put this delicately? – was somewhat well endowed. Viewers had been alerted to its presence by Caitlin Moran of *The Times*, who tweeted to her hundreds of thousands of followers: 'I've just seen a preview tape of tomorrow's *Great British Bake Off*, and forty-one minutes in, there's a shot of a squirrel with ENORMOUS testicles.' The two seconds of him staring into the lens with his, um, nuts there for all to see proved so bizarrely popular that it was included in the next four series. When it was dropped from the 2016 show, it prompted outrage. (*The Sun* was typically restrained: '*Great British Bake Off* replaces saucy squirrel mascot with plucky pheasant – and fans go nuts'). Even the bakers who appeared in the series were mesmerized by it, as Simon Blackwell attests: 'The squirrel with his nuts out! It was probably the first thing I noticed, and it was the first thing my wife and both my children noticed. Good Lord, he was blessed. . .' A YouTube video of the squirrel has been viewed nearly half a million times.

Mel was once asked when she realized the show was going to be big. 'It was when the squirrel went viral,' she replied. 'And I thought, 'Hang on, ooh, we're on to something.'

*

After series one, the programme-makers had gone away to decide what worked and what didn't. 'Series one is your pilot series. You improve it, hope you get it right in series two and stick with that,' a show insider says. The dedicated *Bake Off* team sat down after series one to discuss the changes that would need to be made. Out went the voiceover man and the multiple locations. In came the showstopper, the star baker concept, Paul and Mary showing viewers what a perfect technical bake should look like, and Mel and Sue striving to say, 'On your marks, get set, bake!' in ever sillier voices. Rob, who had also applied for the first series but narrowly missed out on a place, noticed the difference in the audition process. 'The first day of the auditions was with Paul and Mary, on camera. I was like, ah, this has cranked it up a little. . .'

The new setting was Valentine's Mansion, a Grade II-listed house in Ilford, Essex, that was built for the widow of the Archbishop of Canterbury in 1696 and was variously a hospital, a sanctuary for refugees during the Second World War, home to Redbridge council's housing department and latterly a wedding venue. The infamous squirrel was not actually welcome on set – a bunch of the little blighters kept making daring raids on the food supplies and tearing their way through the packaging. From series three onwards, ingredients were decanted into squirrel-proof plastic boxes.

*

Heart-throb Rob was joined by the *Bake Off*'s youngest and oldest bakers so far: Jason, a nineteen-year-old engineering student and member of his university baking society, and Janet, a sixty-three-year-old teacher and grandmother. Janet rapidly became one of the show's most popular contestants – hence her being invited back for the Christmas special – and her fans included Mary's young granddaughters: 'I had one phone call, absolutely sobbing. "Granny, why did you send Janet home? You're wrong!"'

Paul said this series had 'upped the ante' with its challenges, and things certainly got off to a bad start for some of the bakers. Keith came last in the technical challenge and needed to pull something out of the bag for day two. 'I might even be relying on a little bit of luck that something goes bad for someone else,' he confided. Keith! The first rule of *Bake Off* is: never wish bad baking on a fellow contestant. He went home at the end of episode one.

Rob's cake drop was that year's big drama in the tent. 'We're not talking like a great episode of *Casualty*, you know, but I think that cake drop made it a bit dramatic and kind of funny. And maybe kind of relatable as well,' he thinks now. 'When you watch programmes like *The Great British Menu*, you're watching chefs, and for them to do these incredible things. You can't relate to that; it's food porn. From that to *Bake Off*: it's like watching Jimi Hendrix then watching a band in a pub at the weekend. It's two different levels.'

Ian Vallance's Twitter bio bills him as 'disastrous contestant on series two of *The Great British Bake Off*' but he made it to week four quite creditably before being voted out. He loved his time on the show even though he's still not quite sure why he entered – baking 'was just a hobby that I got a bit carried away with.' He sums up the stress of baking against the clock thus: 'Take something you do for relaxation: so you might have a glass of wine in the bath listening to Radio 4 on a Sunday afternoon. Lovely. But it's like being told to do that with somebody screaming at you with a loud hailer to hurry up. I think I described it in one of the interviews as "like the WI on crack". And I remember someone saying, "That's great, could you say that again, but instead of 'crack' could you say 'adrenaline'?".'

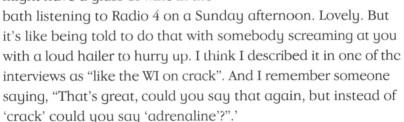

Jo Wheatley had her own way of dealing with the stress. While the other contestants stayed together in a hotel, she was allowed to spend the night before filming at home because she had childcare responsibilities ('I'm an early freak, so once they found out I was never late they let me sleep at home the first night, just not the middle night in case I ran for the hills'). Jo would get up at 5 a.m. on the morning of filming and bake something in her kitchen, in total peace and quiet. 'I found that really calmed my nerves. So I would take muffins or something for the crew to eat, just because I wanted to bake something without any constraints set on me. I knew in an hour's time I was going to be under strict timings and all of those things.'

Jo was a mother of three sons and a grandmother at forty-one. She came across as sweet, nervous and lacking in confidence. 'I've been a mum and a wife,' she said on the show. 'And then *Bake Off* came along and it was the first thing I'd ever done totally for me.' Although contestants were given a list of all the signature and showstopper themes in advance of the show, she only ever practised a week ahead because she didn't want to jinx it.

She had made it to the final with Mary-Anne, a majestically unfazed former rugby player, and Holly, who juggled bringing up two young children with obsessive baking practice. Holly was the bookies' favourite and Mary-Anne the fans' favourite. But it was Jo, the underdog, who triumphed. Everyone on set adored Jo and the team were delighted when she won. To mark her victory, she was presented with a trophy in the shape of a giant bauble filled with whisks. It was changed for the next series for two reasons: the cup was pretty hideous and Love wanted to give the winning baker something they could keep and use. For series three and beyond, they were given a cake stand.

So what is it like to win *The Great British Bake Off*? How does it feel to hear your name announced after one of those epic pauses beloved of reality show directors? 'I genuinely thought they were doing it in reverse order. So when they called my name I thought I was third, but then I looked around and saw my kids jumping up and down and thought, oh God, I've won!'

It was something of an anti-climax for Jo, though. 'Afterwards I got in the car and the kids were like, "That was good, wasn't it?" And then they said, "What's for dinner?"' The show is filmed in May and June but the series doesn't begin airing until August, and the final is not broadcast until October. So the winner has to go back to normal life and keep their victory a secret. 'You know when you have that build-up to Christmas? It's like that. You do all the build-up and you win and it's lovely that day, but the next day it's just surreal because you haven't got to get up and practise your bakes. It's almost like it didn't happen. Your life goes back to relative normality until the quarter-finals are shown, and people start to recognize you.

'The day after the semi-final I was in Marks & Spencer in the queue, and this woman said, "Oh, you're that lady from *Bake Off*, aren't you?" I said, "Yeah, hi." She said, "I'm sorry you went out last night." I said, "No, I didn't," and she said, "Are you sure?"'

When the final was shown, of course, everything changed for Jo. She was inundated with job offers, signed up with Mary Berry's agent and went on to become a best-selling cookery writer.

THE FLAVOURS

This was the year of the Sachertorte, a nineteenth-century Viennese chocolate cake, and an indication that the show would be looking to increasingly elaborate and obscure European bakes for the technical challenge section of the show. The bakers also had to make millefeuilles, a layered mousse cake, croquembouche (a mountain of choux pastry balls drizzled with caramel) and macarons. Things were getting a bit fancier.

The series kicked off with signature cupcakes, using a variety of flavour combinations that read like a list of luxury shower gels: rhubarb and custard, ginger and fig, apple and cinnamon, raspberries and cream, cardamom and orange, banana and toffee, and blackberry and vanilla (with liquorice frosting – Rob couldn't have picked something more divisive if he'd smeared them with an inch of Marmite). The bakers also added creative ingredients to chocolate cake: sour cream, strawberries, raspberries and courgette all made an appearance.

Sweet bakes get all the love, but the quiches in series two sound scrumptious: chorizo, pepper and Gruyère; Stilton, spinach and new potato; smoked bacon and kale; smoked haddock and watercress.

There was no place for lemon in the meringue showstopper – the judges called for something a little less predictable – so in came plums, rhubarb, lime and raspberry. Mary-Anne, though, was especially inventive. No stewed fruit for her. Instead she came up with the Midnight Meringue, so named because lemon meringue reminded her of fluffy clouds on a sunny day and she wanted to produce the opposite. So her recipe had dark chocolate pastry, mocha custard filling and a cooked Italian meringue made with brown sugar. Mary-Anne had a knack for giving her creations intriguing names such as her Everlasting Syllabub, not a recipe from Enid Blyton's *The Magic Faraway Tree* but so called because it keeps in the fridge for several days.

THE UNSUNG HEROES OF THE TENT

The fifty-strong crew on *Bake Off* not only includes the director, producers, camera operators and sound technicians, but also a team of home economists and food producers. Look closely in some of the early episodes and you can glimpse them in the tent, making sure everything is running smoothly.

It is the team's responsibility to ensure each contestant has all the ingredients they need, which they can stockpile because the bakers must send in their signature and showstopper recipes in advance. So they do the big shop to end all big shops, using local suppliers where possible, and buying online if the product is particularly obscure. Series four winner Frances Quinn had 124 ingredients for her cake in the final, a record for the show. Bakers can specify a brand, but the viewers will never know which one is used. Part of the home economists' job is to painstakingly remove every label. The BBC could not be seen to favour Waitrose sultanas.

One of the team, Faenia Moore, told the BBC's *Good Food Magazine* that she stations a junior member of staff outside the nearest supermarket on the weekend of filming 'so I can call and say, "We need more raspberries in ten minutes – go, go, go!"'

Before filming starts, the team tests all the equipment, baking a Victoria sponge in each oven at the same time to check there are no discrepancies. The bakers get a lightning-quick run-through of how everything works, but this doesn't prevent the odd mishap – more than once, a baker has forgotten to turn the oven on. 'I make sure everything is going as smoothly as possible. But if I see a contestant doing something that I know will go wrong, I just have to turn away – I worry that they'll see my reaction and realize.' Instead, she quietly informs the team of the unfolding disaster; the presenters are deployed, and a camera crew is sent to capture the moment. . .

In 2016 there was uproar at the revelation that the technical bake Paul and Mary showed to viewers was not in fact made by them but by the team. 'Great British Fake Off,' thundered *The Sun*. The paper was furious. 'The wholesome BBC bubble is beginning to burst,' it rumbled. But that was surely no surprise to most viewers. The pair are there to judge, not to bake and ice a tennis cake.

'[The crew] really are the unsung heroes of *Bake Off*,' says Diana Beard, who appeared in series five. 'If you wanted another bowl, or if something went wrong and you needed another half a dozen eggs or two lemons, it was there in minutes. And if they'd forgotten something that was on your list of requirements, they'd rush off to the supermarket in Newbury before the programme started and get what they'd missed out.'

And what happens to all that food? Sometimes the team will make up a 'bakers' basket' so the contestants can tuck into each other's creations. Any leftovers are snaffled by the crew – and Mel and Sue, of course, who are also not averse to stealing ingredients from under the bakers' noses in the middle of filming.

Bake a cake in your own kitchen and you'll be faced with a mountain of washing-up. Yet those lovely workstations in the *Bake Off* tent are miraculously free of mess. What happens to that bowl smeared with the remains of a chocolate ganache, or the mixer that five minutes earlier was filled with gloop?

It's really a tale of two tents. There is the one we see on screen, and hidden behind a curtain is another housing the prep kitchen and washing-up area. It has a tray for each baker, bearing the ingredients they have pre-ordered for their signature and showstopper bakes, alongside mountains of basics such as flour, sugar and eggs. On the other side is a bank of television monitors where the director can get an overview of the action, if that's what you can call a group of amateur bakers quietly slaving away at a roulade.

The washing-up is done by hired pot washers, aided by the runners on the show (the most junior members of the production team, and the most hard-working), who are constantly whipping the dirty plates and bowls and spatulas away from the bakers and ferrying them to the makeshift kitchen. There are no

dishwashers, because they would make too much noise, so everything is done by hand. The washer-upper for the later series in the grounds of Welford Park is a village local who gets through eighty sponges and thirty litres of washing up liquid by the time the final comes around. For series three and four at Harptree Court it was a young family friend of the owners.
'I told her they were looking for someone to wash up, and so she came and had a ball,' says Harptree's Linda Hill. 'And there was masses of washing up – it never stopped. The turnaround for the washing up was extraordinary. She used to go home at night and say, "I've inhaled so much icing sugar!"'

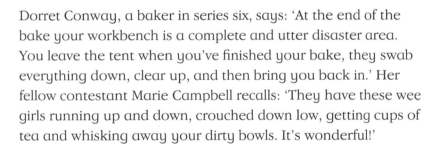

Dorret Conway, a baker in series six, says: 'At the end of the bake your workbench is a complete and utter disaster area. You leave the tent when you've finished your bake, they swab everything down, clear up, and then bring you back in.' Her fellow contestant Marie Campbell recalls: 'They have these wee girls running up and down, crouched down low, getting cups of tea and whisking away your dirty bowls. It's wonderful!'

The weather can be a problem and aeroplanes overhead mean interviews and links often have to be reshot. On the days when it is wet, rather a lot of days considering the programme is filmed in an English May, the sound of rain hammering on the tent is a nightmare for the sound technicians. Cold days are bad for bread, hot days disastrous for chocolate and – as would become evident in Baked Alaska-gate – ice cream. But we'll get to that later.

SERIES 3

BOYS
WHO
BAKE

THE CONTESTANTS

Brendan Lynch,
63, recruitment
consultant from
Sutton Coldfield

Cathryn Dresser,
27, shop assistant
from West Sussex

Daniele Bryden,
45, intensive care
consultant from
Sheffield

James Morton,
21, medical student
from the Shetland
Islands

John Whaite,
23, law student from
Wigan

Manisha Parmar,
36, nursery worker
from Leicester

Natasha Stringer, 36, midwife from Tamworth, Staffordshire

Peter Maloney, 43, sales manager from Windsor, Berkshire

Ryan Chong, 38, photographer from Bristol

Sarah-Jane Willis, 28, vicar's wife from West Sussex

Victoria Chester, 50, CEO of a conservation organization, Somerset

Stuart Marston-Smith, 26, PE teacher from Lichfield, Staffordshire

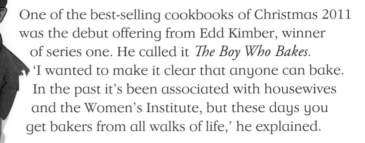

One of the best-selling cookbooks of Christmas 2011 was the debut offering from Edd Kimber, winner of series one. He called it *The Boy Who Bakes*. 'I wanted to make it clear that anyone can bake. In the past it's been associated with housewives and the Women's Institute, but these days you get bakers from all walks of life,' he explained.

Men, young and old, were being inspired by the programme to get baking. Rob from series two recalls a visit to his local pub after his shows had aired. 'We had a pint or two, I was leaving and a guy and a girl stood up and the guy said to me, "Just to let you know, we really loved you on *Bake Off* and we're actually going home to make a cake." That was amazing!'

The sight of men unabashedly icing their Chelsea buns was one of the joys of the programme. Alongside Rob in series two were Simon Blackwell, a rugby coach who now goes by the Twitter handle @buff_baker, fashioning a cupcake holder in the shape of a flower bouquet, and Keith Batsford, with his Mohawk and multiple tattoos, making a cake featuring the Chuggington trains from CBeebies. In series seven, Selasi turned out a batch of raspberry prosecco fondant fancies with Barbie-pink sponge and piped roses.

And by the end of series three in 2012, there was an all-male final. Two of the finalists were students, and studying for the kind of degrees that require hours of hard work every day. John Whaite was a twenty-three-year-old law student, James Morton a twenty-one-year-old medical students. They were joined by Brendan Lynch, a recruitment consultant and the oldest baker in the competition at sixty-three, with a habit of draping a tea towel nattily over his shoulder.

John thought he had two career options before the show. He had started working for the Royal Bank of Scotland, but was not enthused about becoming a banker. It was better than being a lawyer, though – he summed up that path as 'become a solicitor, work, die'. James really did want to be a doctor. But how did he find the time to practise his bakes? The latter stages of the competition coincided with his end-of-year exams, so James found himself perfecting his bakes all week, appearing on the show at weekends for twelve hours at a time, then doing an exam on a Monday morning. Yet he passed, and claimed juggling the two had helped his time management. James got a first-class degree. One of the wonders of *Bake Off* is how the contestants manage to hold down a job as a doctor/builder/prison governor/space satellite designer – space satellite designer! – while practising twenty bakes and taking part in a TV show at the weekends while most of us can barely organize ourselves to do a supermarket shop.

James's bakes had their own crazy genius. He put parsnips in his pear and pecan upside down cake. There was a choux pastry bicycle. In Biscuit Week he made a gingerbread barn, and when it started to collapse he fashioned some caramel cobwebs and called it a haunted barn. The judges thought so too, because that week he was crowned star baker. Not that he was the only inventive contestant. Victoria Chester pulled out all the stops in episode one with a 'blackbird hidden in a pie' cake.

James took loaves of his home-baked bread to freshers' week parties instead of booze. 'When I came to university I realized bread

is very cheap and it's really quite cool,' he said. 'If you come in and you've got bread, everyone's like, "Oh my God, I wanna be friends with you." If this jars with your idea of students living on a diet of baked beans, ropey takeaway kebabs and Pot Noodles, you've failed to move with the times. Students love baking. Rare is the British university that does not have a baking society. Durham has cake crawls instead of bar crawls, visiting cafés to sample their baked goods. Cardiff has GBBO screenings. Leeds has a motto: 'cake is the answer no matter what the question'. Manchester has managed to secure former *Bake Off* contestants as guest speakers. Southampton has gone niche, with a Cake Decorating Society. London School of Economics advertises a proper AGM to decide who organizes their bakes. And Aberdeen University has their own baking competition where students put their signature bakes and showstoppers to the judging panel.

Mary Berry was invited to speak at the Oxford Union before a packed house, where questions from the students included how to get a sponge to stop sinking in the middle. 'Whenever a series of *Bake Off* is on, we get more members,' says Katie Murray, twenty-two, president of the University of East Anglia Baking Society, which was set up in 2014 as a direct result of interest in the show. Tea-room crawls are a mid-term highlight: 'Norwich has some lovely tea rooms, so we go round them having cake and coffee.' Each week, members take along a bake that has been made to fit a *Bake Off* theme. 'Last year we had judging, like they do on the show, but we found that put people off. Now we've taken the judging element out and we just sit and chat and share each other's bakes.'

Of course not every student knocks up a poppy seed loaf in between seminars. 'It depends on the person. I do know a lot of people who do stick to jacket potatoes. But at the same time, I know lots who enjoy baking a cake, because it's quite de-stressing.'

Durham University has its own star baker: Michael Georgiou, an economics and politics student who was a contestant in series seven. He did a talk and baking demonstration for Durham's baking society, and the event sold out in five minutes. 'We also did a screening of the *Bake Off* final where people brought their own bakes. We put it on the big screen at the student union – the first time that a non-sporting event had been shown there. We got about 100 people,' says Rachael Smith, the society's president.

'We do a big variety of things. We've quite a lot of students come who have no baking knowledge, no baking ability, so we try and do things that are quite inclusive, like workshops teaching people how to bake. And we do try and have a few events that are very simple, calming things around exam time, for example icing biscuits and cakes.'

Bake Off has democratized baking, she thinks. 'It makes it not seem as privileged. It's not just for middle-class, middle-aged people to do in their kitchen at home. You get so many different people on it, you learn about their lives and their backgrounds. I think sometimes there's a snobbery that seems to be attached to baking. You think to be really good at baking you've got to be sixty and a member of the Women's Institute and make your own jam. That's why I like the younger contestants, like Martha and Flora, because it helps to make it seem a bit cooler.'

*

Series three had a new location: Harptree Court, a Georgian house set in fifty-five glorious acres. The location manager had been tasked with finding 'a field with a vista' to pitch the tent and after a lengthy search discovered Harptree, with its stunning views across the Chew Valley and a little balustraded bridge over a stream. For weeks, the show took over the lives of owners Linda and Charles Hill. Linda was always on hand to provide tea, sympathy and a restorative glass of wine on 'eviction' day.

'We got to know them so well because they were living in our house, practically – not actually staying, but they'd arrive at 6.30 in the morning and quite often not go until the early hours. And when they're sitting in a room opposite your kitchen and you're giving them tea and coffee and TLC, you do get to see their good bits and their bad bits and their excitement and their disappointment,' says Linda.

The crew took over the house, even though the Hills kept on running the house as a B&B throughout filming. One room became the production office, and another upstairs a 'green room' for Mary, Paul, Mel and Sue to relax when they weren't needed in the tent. 'They took over, but in the nicest possible way. It was just like having family come to visit. My grandchild would be in a highchair and Mel would feed her; Sue played with the dogs. We were very much part of that family and we loved every minute of it. We couldn't have got to know them all better if we tried.

'We had weeks of absolute magic. Sue and Mel, I have to say, are the funniest people I have ever met in my entire life. Genuinely, my stomach and my cheekbones hurt from laughing when they left.' A wooden bread board has pride of place in the Hills' kitchen – a thank you from the production team, bearing the message: 'GBBO – love from Love'.

For the Hills, despite the upheaval, it was a complete joy – not least because they got to eat some of the leftover bakes. Linda, who can make a mean lemon drizzle cake of her own, became a de facto crew member. 'And whereas everybody else put on weight, I lost weight [laughs] even though I ate everything that was in the tent, because I was running backwards and forwards and doing so much for everybody.' When the show moved to a new location, 'I was quite sad I thought oh, my half stone's never going to go again!'

Did she join in and shed a tear each Sunday when a baker left? 'Oh, gosh, yes. I would always have a glass of wine ready for them, you know, because I sort of felt they needed that before they went off. They needed a bit of a hug and a sit down. . .'

Watch carefully and you may be able to spot Linda's husband trundling into shot. 'We have a tree house for self-catering guests in the middle of the woods. So Charles would go down with his trolley to take stuff down there, and bring the old stuff up. The crew would say, "Oh, God, here comes Charles again." But with something like you can't say 'Cut' so he's either edited in or edited out, but when he's in you can't miss him.'

Custardgate and Bingate were yet to come, but an even greater disaster was narrowly averted in series three: Spanielgate. 'The thing that worried us the most was, were the dogs going to get into the tent?' remembers Linda. 'They're springers. Fast. And there was one point where my husband manhandled one of them literally as they were about to get into the tent. Sue thought that would have been hysterical. It would have been an absolute disaster.'

*

Series three did have one big drama. If you switched on your telly in the middle of Pastry Week, you'd have been forgiven for thinking you'd stumbled across a particularly gory episode of *Casualty*, after John cut his finger on an electric mixer while trying to make a strudel. The resulting bloodbath resembled the closing scenes of *Carrie*, but it does help when one of your fellow bakers is an intensive care consultant, and Danny [Daniele] was there to administer first aid. John exited the tent, finger bandaged and arm in a sling, lamenting the fact he had to leave because 'my strudel's going to be amazing'. Rather than penalize him for not finishing, the producers decided that no one would be eliminated that week.

The stress was getting to John, though. The following week, he snapped after Paul criticized his Chelsea buns. 'I was exhausted – I'd cut my finger the week before so I couldn't knead the dough properly,' he revealed afterwards. 'I felt like Paul didn't give any constructive criticism, so after the cameras rolled I approached him outside the tent and almost squared up to him.' Crikey! Luckily, Paul took it in his stride: 'He actually spoke to me very kindly, like I was his teenage son, and told me not to worry about it.'

The all-male final helped to normalize the idea of men baking. Richard Burr, from series five, used to cringe at 'the idea that you had to be almost extra-geezerly to counteract the feminizing effect of baking' on TV. 'If I'm doing book signings or just walking down the road, you'll get a big, hairy geezer coming along saying, "My wife loves the show, she watches it." But then he'll be able to list things you've made. Giving fellas permission to go and make a cake is nice. Because from a boring, serious point of view, it's important that men share the responsibility and see baking as something that's fun to do. Because it's lovely. I love that side of it, that men do it. I kind of feel a little bit sad that I was considered to be someone who got men into the kitchen, because men should be doing that anyway. I was doing a book signing last week and this fella came up to me with his wife and said, "We've been married years and I got your book and this last year I've been baking in the kitchen and it's been great." I couldn't have been happier for his wife. As long as he washes up after he makes the cake.'

Mark Onley, a kitchen fitter, appeared in series four. 'I think it's seen as a predominantly female world, although there are a lot more men doing it now. But personally – apart from the people I met on telly and the people I see on telly, I don't know any men who bake cakes. None of my male friends bake cakes. I suppose it's quite tricky to get cakes right and stuff; there's a lot of effort, you've got to be precise with ingredients and baking times.'

That three men had made the final guaranteed column inches, but Mary insisted this wasn't intentional. She told *Good Food Magazine*: 'When it comes to the judging, my friends are surprised that we have complete control over who stays and who goes. That's why we might get three girls in a final, or three boys – maybe it's not great television, but that's just what happened.'

Despite doing so much to get men baking, the programme was to drop a clanger in series seven by putting out promotional pictures of the contestants that featured pink icing for the women and blue icing for the men. That gender stereotyping went down like a lead balloon with fans, who tweeted their dismay alongside the #everydaysexism hashtag. The BBC later digitally altered the images to colour the icing purple, green and yellow.

Still, we've come a long way. It's only in the past few decades that men have really cooked at all, and that didn't come about entirely out of choice. As Dr Annie Gray, food historian, explains: 'The big change came in the 1960s and 1970s. Up until then, the woman of the house was doing the cooking. Men just didn't go in the kitchen, unless it was a bachelor pad and then they might cook a chop. The growing women's rights movement changed things, and the financial pressure of both parties needing to work; otherwise they couldn't afford a house.

'But most everyday cooking is still done by women, especially by mothers. You see that really appallingly employed by popular culture. Men cooking is represented by them barbecuing something, which is a hobby they do at the weekend.'

Writing in 2016, Edd Kimber (series 1) said the stereotype of the 'bloke baker' still persisted – knocking out bread and pies rather than cakes. But he praised *Bake Off* for doing its bit 'by putting men front and centre of the show, in that quaint and twee tent. Finally we are starting to see male bakers come out from the shadows.' He hopes that 'in years' time, we won't even have to talk about baking in gender terms. You can either make great food or you can't. End of story.'

*

'The musk of testosterone and icing sugar in the tent is very, very, heavy,' intoned Mel, as she introduced the all-male final. The signature bake was a pithivier – a pie, by another name, but that doesn't sound quite as impressive – which provided the perfect opportunity for some Mel and Sue punning ('Time's up. I mean it. I'm not taking the pithivier'). Even Paul joined the innuendo-fest (telling John: 'I just hope your rough puff rises to the occasion').

Things didn't start well for James, who had the dreaded soggy bottom. But he turned it around in the technical challenge, which was about as unmanly a cake as the producers could dream up: pink fondant fancies. James won, although Mary noted that none of them had done terribly well. Surely now it was his final to lose? So it was on to the showstopper. The trio were tasked with making a chiffon cake – a cloudlike sponge of oil and egg-white batter – inspired by their own personal highlight of the year.

Brendan's almond-coated raspberry chiffon cake, topped with a giant heart and decorated with fresh raspberries, had a touching backstory. It was a family reunion cake, he explained, because 2012 was the year that members of his family who had been separated for three decades finally healed their differences.

John opted for a heaven and hell cake, with a dark chocolate and orange hell beneath a lemon and coconut meringue heaven. The hell represented his finals, the heaven was the birth of his nephew.

And James? Well, in a move that with hindsight looks like complete lunacy, he decided to make five cakes. F.I.V.E. The middle one would have a Union Jack and the other four would represent the various bits of the United Kingdom. The perils of trying to bake five cakes on a workstation barely big enough for one became evident when he had to balance one cake tin on a stool and it promptly fell off, sending its contents spilling to the floor.

Displaying exactly the kind of calm that you would hope to find in a hospital doctor, James simply murmured: 'Ohhh. . . that's my cake,' before making another one. But when it came to the judging, we instantly knew that James was out of the running. The five separate cakes turned out to be. . . five separate cakes, sitting next to each other, which did not impress Paul. The crumb was dry. Mary declared it 'a bit cakey', which sounds like it should be a compliment but evidently isn't. She did offer a bit of her trademark 'look on the bright side' commentary – 'There's plenty of cake for a party, and we're having a fête, so you're the main contributor!' – but it was clear that poor James had fallen at the final hurdle.

John had been busy melting the chocolate on his cake with a hairdryer, and thought he'd done as well as he could. 'I came, I saw, I baked. And hopefully I conquered,' he said. Brendan was overcome with emotion after finishing his bake, telling the cameras that a win 'would be an extraordinary endorsement of what I've achieved over the decade'.

And before we knew it, it was time to announce the winner. It was John. 'The passion that the guy has is just phenomenal,' Paul said. John hugged his mum, the mum who had taught him to bake, and said with a tear in his eye: 'My mum's so proud and that's the biggest prize I've got out of this – my mum being happy with me. It just means the absolute world to me.' He also told her that he wasn't going be a banker.

*

John and Edd Kimber were the star bookings at the following year's Women's Institute Christmas Fair and Real Jam Festival. This venerable organization has been going since 1915 and received a boost in 2003 from the film *Calendar Girls* – remember Celia Imrie sparing her blushes behind those iced buns? – but nothing had prepared them for the *Bake Off* effect. Between 2010 and 2013, membership grew by a quarter to over 211,000, the highest since the 1970s.

Ruth Bond, then chairwoman of the National Federation of Women's Institutes, said *Bake Off* had inspired women to take up baking by 'taking away the fear factor' and making it look fun. The current chair, Janice Langley, says now: 'Home baking has been enjoying a great resurgence over the past few years and many new WI members have told us that brushing up on their baking skills was one of the reasons why they decided to join. Baking is something that has been associated with the WI since its beginnings and many members are experts in their field, but it is wonderful to see so many people becoming inspired to try baking at home.' When a new branch opened in Bristol in 2013, 350 women queued around the block and 130 had to be turned away.

The country appeared to be in the grip of baking fever. Lynn Hill had retired from a job in a bank when she decided to launch a cake club. The idea came to her a year before she had hosted a pop-up afternoon tea event in her front room in Leeds, and people loved it.

'I was going to do a one-off and get it out of my system. I even cancelled some events because I got nervous. I thought, how can I have total strangers in my house? But I did the one event and it went really well. I thought, maybe I can tap into this. . .' So the Clandestine Cake Club was born. Book a space, and you're sent details of the secret location. The first meet-up in December 2010 was in an empty office, with a plastic parrot as a signpost for those in the know. Eleven people turned up and, Lynn says, 'we had the best time ever'.

The timing could not have been more perfect. As *Bake Off* grew in popularity, so did the Clandestine Cake Club. Soon, meetings were springing up all over the shop – more than 200 around the world. There are clubs in Spain, Japan, America, Canada, Australia and New Zealand. There is even one in Myanmar (Burma). Membership is free, and there is only one rule: you have to take a cake. Cupcakes, muffins, brownies, pies and tarts are strictly prohibited.

'The whole cake rule is the only rule. And it's crucial, because conversations begin when you cut the first slice,' explains Lynn. 'One day I'd love to do an experiment: get two different tables, one set up with a whole cake, the other with cupcakes and little things. I'm pretty sure that the people from the table with the whole cake would be talking to each other more. Because with a cake, you have to say to the other person, 'Would you like a slice? Can you pass me a knife please? Isn't it nice inside!' But with cupcakes, there's no reason for anyone to speak to each other.'

Lynn was approached by a literary agent and has written two recipe books. Running the club is now a full-time job, and there are 19,000 members. 'I had no idea it would turn into something as big as this. When *Bake Off* comes along, that's when interest shows again because people start Googling bake clubs and cake clubs, and they find us.'

Every series brought a deluge of press releases from supermarkets and retailers, detailing how the *Bake Off* effect had boosted sales of everything from cake stands to goldenberries (Waitrose saw a 180 per cent goldenberries sales spike in 2015 after Tamal used them in his biscuits). In 2016, Morrisons announced the appointment of a dedicated 'bake officer' to monitor the show and ensure stores were fully stocked with the necessary ingredients. A range of *Great British Bake Off* official merchandise was launched, and quickly became one of the top-sellers at kitchenware shop Lakeland, where sales of Anti Gravity Cake Kits were to fly off the shelves after Nadiya used one to construct her Fizzy Pop Cheesecake in series six. Paul Hollywood brought out his own baking range, selling branded dough cutters and brownie tins.

As early as 2012, John Lewis was reporting a 33 per cent increase in the sale of bread-makers after *Bake Off* did Bread Week. 'We are definitely noticing a trend for homemade bread-baking,' the store said. 'It is now incredibly fashionable, with TV shows such as *The*

Great British Bake Off encouraging us to bake our own.' Annual sales of home-baking products rose from £523 million in 2009 to £1.7 billion in 2014, according to market researchers Mintel. Norman Calder, star of series five, says people certainly caught the baking bug in his town. 'When I was on *Bake Off* I spoke to the manager of my local Tesco and he said, "Since you've been on this show we've sold a huge amount of flour, baking powder, eggs, all sorts of stuff." Where *Bake Off* has succeeded is introducing people throughout the country to baking. I like to think the whole idea of *Bake Off* is that you get on the telly, people watch it and say, "Christ, I could do better than that. I'll have a go."'

Rose Prince cautions not to get too carried away with the sales figures. 'I'm certain it inspires people to bake, and when you go into one of the big supermarkets you will see they now have much greater baking ranges. There's no doubt they have more on offer; they're selling things like gelatin, yeast, good vanilla. But I can't believe those sales come anywhere near to even a small proportion of the viewers that the programme attracts.'

She does think *Bake Off* came along at exactly the right time. 'I think it was a combination of emerging social media but also the timing itself, just post the financial crash, when people found themselves staying in more and becoming interested in home pursuits. And I think cooking, and baking particularly for its comfort element, fitted perfectly.'

The show tapped into the idea that baking has become a relaxing, mindful pastime (mindfulness being one of the decade's great trends – the WI now runs residential 'Mindful Baking' courses). Go back to the first half of the century and people would have been baffled by the idea of baking for pleasure. 'At any point when you don't have to do something, it's a hobby,' says Annie Gray. 'We don't regard baked goods as an essential part of our meal. A cake is not necessary. In the 1930s, your quintessential British meal was meat and two veg followed by a pudding. Two, if not three, courses was the norm. Now it's one course, maybe two if you invite people over for dinner. But even then a pudding is not necessarily baked. It might be ice cream, and it might be something you can buy, because baking is regarded as fiddly and time consuming. The first thing to go when there was a movement out of the kitchen was baking.

'The artisan bread movement has taken things full circle, as a backlash against the white sliced loaf manufactured via the industrial Chorleywood process, which produces bread with maximum efficiency and plenty of additives. But it's very much a class lifestyle choice, the same as going to farmers' markets. It's brilliant that people are going out and buying bread but at the end of the day it's something you pay money for. The term "artisan" in France still means something very specific. Here, you have McDonalds claiming to do "artisan" bread. I mean, really?'

Bake Off's homemade, homespun aesthetic had caught the public mood, and the creative heads at Love Productions could see the potential for similarly themed shows. So 2013 saw the launch of *The Great British Sewing Bee*, in which a bunch of talented amateurs competed to make shift dresses and pussy bow blouses; and 2015 brought *The Great Pottery Throwdown* where talented hopefuls created porcelain tea sets and strawberry pots.

And while *Bake Off* most definitely did not chime with the clean eating brigade, it did promote the idea of getting back to basics by using natural ingredients. Look on the box of a supermarket Victoria sandwich and you find a list of strange-sounding chemicals. Make your own and all you need are eggs, sugar, butter, flour baking powder and jam. In a seemingly complicated modern world, the simplicity of *Bake Off* was a large part of its charm.

THE
FLAVOURS

Pineapple upside down cake is a family favourite, but if you're a *Bake Off* contestant I'm afraid tinned pineapple rings aren't going to cut it. Hence the signature upside down cakes featured sour cherry and walnut, apple and hazelnut, plum and ginger, pear and pecans with parsnip (a slightly left-field choice from James) and the even more left-field kumquat and polenta combination from Ryan Chong.

Another enduring family classic, the meringue, popped up in Desert Week. Fig, chestnut and cherry. Strawberry, rose and pistachio. Pear, chocolate and hazelnut. Gooseberry, almond and honey. Only Stuart Marston-Smith went for the inventive name, with the stupendous-sounding Choca Blocka Mocha Meringue.

This series also saw a Wellington signature challenge. Vegetarians: look away now. Cathryn Dresser won with a Full English Wellington, which comprised sausages, black pudding, Parma ham, quails' eggs, mushrooms and tomatoes. James's contribution was an artery- hardening Four Pig Wellington.

James hailed from Scotland, and was determined to feature regional recipes. So he gave us tattie scones and clootie dumplings – the former made with potato and sometimes served with a cooked breakfast, the latter resembling a Christmas pudding made with flour, breadcrumbs, dried fruit and suet. He also served up banana and clove puddings, which are not Scottish in the slightest but do sound a bit odd.

TOUGHEST TECHNICAL BAKES.

Look back at the first series and the list of technical bakes reads like a list of treats from your local bakery. Victoria sandwich. Scones. Cornish pasties. But as every year went by, and the show's food producer had to scour the history books for new ideas, the technicals became ludicrously complex – though at least they gave Mel and Sue the chance to try out some very bad foreign accents. Dampfnudel, anyone?

Kouign-amann: if you've never heard of this and can't pronounce it, you're not alone – none of the bakers had either (series 5). It's an obscure yeasted pastry from Brittany, made from rolled-out dough layered with butter and sugar. Apparently, Bretons traditionally serve them with a glass of cider after Sunday lunch.

*

Tennis cake: featuring in Victorian Week (series 6), this marzipan-covered fruit cake tested the bakers' decorative skills by asking them to fashion a tennis court out of icing. Mat Riley learned the hard way that choosing Fungus the Bogeyman green and baking your royal icing in the oven were not the way to victory.

*

Jumbles: Victorian Week was replaced a series later by Tudor Week (series 7). Yes, the cuisine responsible for Henry VIII's gout was celebrated on *Bake Off*, but these were really quite restrained: biscuits flavoured with caraway seeds and twisted into a knot.

*

Sachertorte: the second series eased
the bakers in with iced fingers, chocolate
roulades and brandy snaps, before chucking
this in for the final: a glossy chocolate
cake invented by Austrian confectioner
Franz Sacher. The bakers had to pipe the
word 'Sacher' on the top; Mary-Anne
Boermans (series 2) piped her daughter's
name, Sacha, by mistake.
She didn't win.

*

Flaounes (s) Paul was familiar with these
cheese-filled Cypriot pastries, traditionally
baked for Easter, because he once worked
as a baker in a Cyprus hotel. But even Mary
confessed she had never heard of mastic
and mehlepi, ingredients included in
his recipe. (series 6)

*

Spanische Windtorte: not Spanish at all,
but Austrian, this complicated construction
involves meringue rings, whipped cream and
soft fruit, and is decorated with crystallized
or fondant violets (series 6).

*

Dampfnudel: a cross between a bread roll
and a steamed dumpling, but sweet and
poached in a mixture of milk, sugar
and butter, this was a *Bake Off* challenge that
didn't call for any actual baking
(series 7). And what do dampfnudel taste
like, Mary? 'Just like an iced bun
without the icing.'

HOW DOES IT FEEL TO BE THE BAKER GOING HOME?

The moment when the presenters – with genuine sadness – announce your *Bake Off* journey is over can be an emotional one. Most bakers admit to feeling gutted.

'I would happily have gone back and made tea for people the following week because I missed being part of it. It's strange, in a way, that it's such a big experience. I got back home and I'd got bags of freeze-dried blackberries that I'd bought ready for the following week's programme, which never got used. And it was ages before I could actually do anything with them. It is a little bit of a downer.' (Howard Middleton, series 4)

'You really do become like a little family. It's hard to say goodbye knowing that they're going to be there next week and you're not.' (Dorret Conway, series 6)

'Once I got home, I felt a bit disappointed the following week. Because I'd been retired for four years from my job, and then this came into my life and it occupied my whole life. And then suddenly I had nothing. I just missed it so much.' (Norman Calder, series 5)

'It was quite hard to get over. It took a while – I couldn't watch the episode. They make you watch it for the follow-up show, *An Extra Slice*, and I said to them, "Is it OK if I don't watch it?" I haven't watched it since. I had a party for the episode where I went out, a big old party, but I still didn't watch it. We just hung out in the kitchen.' (Kate Henry, series 5)

'The week when I left it wasn't going to plan and I kind of had my suspicions that I would be going home. So it didn't come as a complete shock. . . But what made me sad, was not the fact I was leaving but the fact that everybody was quite sad that I was leaving.' (Chetna Makan, series 5)

'You have to wear it. When they called out my name I didn't have any feeling of, "Hold on a second, let's look at the facts here!" It's just the emotion, because you're such a fan of the show, and you always feel sorry for the person who goes home first. You're instantly ushered off and you're mic'd up again and there's a camera crew asking you, "How do you feel?" And you're thinking, don't cry on national TV! Keep it together! There might have been a solitary tear in the bathroom.' (Stu Henshall, series 6)

Some bakers – only the male ones, mind you – insist they felt some relief to be going home. 'I'm six foot two. Sitting on those stools I was just thinking, I have back ache and I want to go home, so thank God for that. I could see my standard of baking wasn't going to keep rising. I did want to stay on, but not as badly as other people.' (Simon Blackwell, series 2)

'I said this on telly and I like to think I would have followed through with it: if they hadn't said to me I was going home, I'd have got up and said, "No, I'm going." Because the people that were on there were in a completely different class of baking. I was almost like Ed Balls on *Strictly*. I'm not saying I'm a hopeless baker, but in terms of where they were and where I was, I was a rank amateur and they were almost professionals. I almost felt they'd picked me by mistake. So I wasn't emotional, I was kind of relieved because if I'd have had to go back again I'd have felt like I was really cheating the system.' (Mark Onley, series 4)

'I was gutted. But, to be honest, I was also knackered.' (Rob Billington, series 2)

THE CONTESTANTS

Ali Imdad,
25, charity worker
from Birmingham

Beca Lyne-
Pirkis, 31, Military
Wives Choir singer
from Aldershot,
Hertfordshire

Christine
Wallace, 66,
company director
from Didcot,
Oxfordshire

Deborah Manger,
51, dentist from
Peterborough

Frances Quinn,
31, children's clothes
designer from
Market Harborough,
Leicestershire

Glenn Cosby,
37, teacher from
Teignmouth, Devon

Howard Middleton, 51, council worker from Sheffield

Kimberley Wilson, 30, psychologist from London

Lucy Bellamy, 38, horticulturist from Grimsby

Mark Onley, 37, carpenter and kitchen fitter from Milton Keynes

Robert Smart, 54, space satellite designer from Melbourn, Cambridgeshire

Ruby Tandoh, 20, student from Southend, Essex

Toby Waterworth, 30, web programmer from Reading

There are lots of considerations when selecting a group of people who must hold the nation's attention on primetime television for ten weeks. They need to be able to bake. They need to be able to bake and talk at the same time. They need to have (as *The X Factor*'s Louis Walsh is fond of putting it) the likeability factor. But plenty more goes into the mix.

Anna Beattie told the *Guardian* in 2015 that it was 'about trying to get a representative mix'. Representative of what, exactly? 'I don't know,' she replied. 'Britain?' The BBC is bound by Royal Charter to represent all the nations and regions of Britain. As a public service broadcaster, it also has the stated aim of 'reflecting modern Britain accurately and authentically', striving to appeal to all age groups and ethnicities. In *Bake Off*, it had a golden opportunity to fulfil that brief. Chetna Makan who appeared in series five observed: 'Having all women, or all the same young, pretty things, is not going to work because then it doesn't appeal to everyone. And I think that's why they get millions and millions of viewers, because everyone's got someone they're rooting for.'

Diversity breeds diversity, because seeing a varied line-up encourages people to apply. 'Because I knew they took from different ethnicities and stuff, I said, well, that means I have got a chance. They're not just going to take white, middle-class people,' says Dorret Conway of series six. 'I thought it was actually worth having a go. They've managed to cut across all ethnic backgrounds, age, sex, in a way no other programme seems to have been able to do.'

An insider says: 'Obviously, you start at the beginning of every *Bake Off* saying, "Let's try and get bakers who we haven't seen before." All our programmes have always been diverse and multicultural. And do we try and give the broad spectrum? Absolutely. From 16 to 105 – if we could get a 105-year-old who was a good enough baker, we absolutely would.'

First and foremost, the contestants must be able to bake. 'This is tested at every level of the application process. It's asked about in the application form, it's tested in the casting call, it's judged in the first audition and then proved in the second.' But they are also looking for bakers who will 'spark conversation', who offer something different from the previous series, and who are distinct from one another in terms of baking style. 'You couldn't have twelve Normans in the tent,' explains one of the casting team in reference to Norman Calder's simple recipes (although what a show that would be).

One senior executive on the show explains the process. 'Whenever you cast any kind of show with more than one or two people, you're looking for a broad spread. A large percentage of people that applied for the show were of exactly the same ilk: thirty-something, slightly bored with their life – it's their equivalent of winning the lottery. Our job was to find different characters. We didn't go in there saying, "We need the gay one with the dog, we need the sixty-year-old." We didn't have boxes to tick. But we're not going to want two gay guys with a dog or three retired schoolteachers. We want different people, and people who are there because they like baking, not because they want fame.'

From a ratings point of view it helps if the bakers have a 'TV personality', according to the team. This can be uncovered at different points in the selection process. The first that producers knew of Nadiya's fantastic facial expressions was during an audition when she thought she had burnt her cake.

And it turns out that not all auditionees are equal. Rob Billington had applied for series one but didn't make the cut. Then, when auditions were underway for series two, he got a phone call saying, 'Have you thought about re-applying for the second series?' She told him that he had got down to the final shortlist for series one. He thinks now that in that first series, 'The "young guy who bakes" box was already ticked – he was Edd Kimber.' Rob decided to re-apply 'because I thought, if I'm being called back, maybe there's a good chance I'll be on this show.' He went through all the audition stages again, and was picked.

Bake Off fans like to sort the bakers into types. For a truly successful series, some or all of the following should be included:

THE MAN WITH A MANLY JOB.

A bloke's bloke, someone you'd imagine more at home with a Black and Decker power drill than a pastry brush. Extra points if they're handsome. So there was Richard Burr (series 5), the builder with a pencil behind his ear; Mat Riley, the fireman (series 6); Mark Onley, the kitchen fitter (series 4); Simon Blackwell, the rugby coach (series 2, and actually only a part-time rugby coach, but the producers listed that as his occupation for maximum man points). This type is best illustrated by Stuart Marston-Smith, the hunky PE teacher from series three. Just to hammer the point home, he was filmed sitting down in a busy school corridor, tracksuit on after a morning on the sports field, leafing through a pink cookbook.

THE LOVELY GRANDMA.

Always smiley, usually blonde. Technically doesn't have to have grandchildren – she's just the dream granny you've always wanted (other than Mary, of course). She's looking for a new challenge now that her career is drawing to a close and her children have flown the nest. In the fourth series this role was filled by Christine Wallace, a glamorous lady with a hint of Felicity Kendall about her. See also: Janet Basu (series 2), Nancy Birtwhistle (series 5), Marie Campbell (series 6), and Val Stones, aka the Cake Whisperer (series 7).

THE YOUNG MUM WHO WANTS TO DO SOMETHING FOR HERSELF.

The queen here is of course Nadiya Hussain, series six winner. She had spent ten years at home raising three young children, before plucking up the courage to enter *Bake Off*. See also: Miranda Gore Brown (series 1), Holly Bell (series 2), Jo Wheatley (series 2), Cathryn Dresser (series 3).

THE NICE YOUNG MAN WHO BRINGS OUT ALL YOUR MOTHERLY TENDENCIES (PLAID SHIRT ESSENTIAL, KNITWEAR A BONUS).

Edd Kimber kicked this off in series one, followed by John Waite and James Morton in series three (they were both students, so probably still brought their washing home at weekends). Andrew Smyth elicited this response from viewers even though he was a qualified engineer who designed jet engines for Rolls Royce (series 7).

The baker who drew most of the attention in series four was Ruby Tandoh, a twenty-year-old student from Southend. She had moments of self-doubt (really, at twenty, who doesn't?) and her emotions were close to the surface, so when her first bake was a mini disaster she couldn't hold back the tears. But whereas the sight of other contestants crying had brought on a wave of viewer sympathy – think back to Mark and his collapsing marmalade cake in the very first episode – when it came to Ruby the response was very different. She was accused of milking it, of overdramatizing, of making doe eyes (or 'dough eyes') at Paul. Even Raymond Blanc, the venerable chef, got involved by complaining that the show was 'awash with female tears'. But along with her baking skills, Ruby also happened to be brilliantly articulate and wrote a piece for the *Guardian* in which she put her critics firmly in their place: 'If I see one more person use the hackneyed, "dough-eyed" pun I will personally go to their house and force-feed them an entire Charlotte Royale.'

Her fellow bakers feel she was unfairly maligned. 'Most of us had cried from time to time. It can be a real pressure-cooker environment,' says Howard. Christine concurs: 'She was a very sweet girl. I really liked Ruby. She was very skilled, trying to do her studying at the same time as baking, and I think it impacted on her a bit. But to be accused of flirting with Paul – well, we never saw any sign of that.'

Ruby later came out as gay and tweeted: 'For those who thought I fancied Paul Hollywood or that I'd ever bang him to get ahead . . . joke's on you, you massive sh***ing misogynists.' Ouch.

A year on, Kate Henry (series 5) found herself cast in the femme fatale role. 'People were saying, "Oh, you're the Ruby character." I was thinking, I'm twenty years older than Ruby! I think the "single female" thing does exist in it.' Sure enough, headlines started appearing which referred to 'The Great British Flirt Off' (groan) between Kate and Paul.

*

Series Four was a turning point for the show. When ratings reached critical mass, it was clear that the show had entered a different league and was destined for primetime BBC1.

At Harptree Court, once again the hosting venue, owner Linda Hill was aware of the change. 'We could see that happening – the popularity. Even when people were talking to us, for the first series it was, "Wow, you've got *The Great British Bake Off*." But by the second series it was, "Oh my God, you've got *The Great British Bake Off*!"

The show had been one of the jewels of BBC2, nurtured by the channel controller, Janice Hadlow. It was her vision that helped to shape it. 'People are in a different frame of mind at eight o'clock,' she once explained. 'They're looking for something that offers them a bit more pleasure, a bit more entertainment.'

But it is an occupational hazard of running BBC2 that if you turn a programme into a hit, BBC1 will come along and nick it.

It had happened with *The Apprentice* and *Who Do You Think You Are?* And, inevitably, it happened with *Bake Off*, when series four pulled in an average of five and a half million viewers and over seven million for the final.

Hadlow put a brave face on it. 'I'm sad to see it go. I won't pretend I'm not,' she said. 'It's been a great show to have. I've loved my time working with it. I think it's one of my favourite shows. It is a condition of being a controller of BBC2 that sometimes you see programmes that you love get on the escalator and move up to the next level.' No doubt through gritted teeth, she described the BBC1 land grab as 'more sharing than stealing'.

Bake Off was considered in the same league as the corporation's Saturday-night juggernaut, *Strictly Come Dancing*, which also had a satellite show of its own. This addition was as much about keeping BBC2 happy as anything else, but it quickly became a firm favourite with the fans. With the *Junior Bake Off*, and the Masterclass shows in which Paul and Mary recreated the bakes as a how-to guide, and various special editions for charity, *Bake Off* was fast becoming an industry.

The celebrity version of *Bake Off* had started in 2012, with a series in aid of Sport Relief. By 2015 it had gone glamorous: as if the presence of Joanna Lumley, Lulu, Jennifer Saunders and Alexa Chung wasn't enough, they'd only gone and got Dame Edna. That series also featured the late Victoria Wood, who made – joy of joys – a Mrs Overall cake.

But 2016 was the icing on the cake (sorry) because, really, where else could you find the prime minister's wife in a vol au vents battle with David James? Samantha Cameron won the star baker apron after Paul pronounced her crab and chilli vol au vents 'absolutely perfect'.

By this point, declaring your love of baking had become the fashionable thing to do. Geri Horner (*née* Halliwell), another contestant on the 2016 Sport Relief series, is a convert. Here she is on Instagram, glazing a lemon tart while listening to a soundtrack of her own music; there she is making a ginger cake (geddit?) with a Union Jack mixer. The whole thing is a work of art. And Alexa Chung, the It Girl's It Girl, may not have switched her oven on in three years – 'I keep my shoes in the oven' – but that didn't stop her snapping up a celebrity *Bake Off* place.

Kate Moss, no less, a woman legendary for her rock'n'roll lifestyle, confided in an interview: 'I make jam and, oh my God, it is so delicious. My signature is damson or quince, and it's called Kate's Sweet and Sticky. Basically, I'm a domestic goddess. I gave it to Jamie Oliver and his kids texted my kid the next day, saying: "Oh, your mum's jam is really good, we just had some and it's better than Dad's." Take that Jamie Oliver.'

*

If Ruby was the most controversial character in this series, then the most beloved was surely Howard. The Sheffield Council worker was just what we want in a *Bake Off* contestant: wry sense of humour, unflappable in a crisis. Google pictures of Howard (go on) and he's smiling in every single one.

Not that Howard likes looking back on his *Bake Off* days. 'I was just appalled at how my chin disappears into my neck! There was a friend who said to me, "Do you realize your chin goes into your neck?" And I was like, "Yes, I'm watching it now." They said, "Ooh, you'll have to bear that in mind next week," and I said, "It's all filmed! It'll be like this every week!" The week that I went out, it was on *Gogglebox*, and the posh couple, Steph and Dom, were debating whether it would be me or Glenn going home. He said, "Oh, Howie, I liked Howie." And she said, "Yes, but he has no chin." And I thought, well, thanks. . .'

Howard was also part of series four's big drama. Because before Bingate (more of that later), there was Custardgate. Deborah Manger, a mild-mannered dental specialist from Northamptonshire, accidentally removed Howard's crème anglaise from the fridge and used it in her trifle. He was wonderfully gracious about it – 'I'm sure one custard is as good as the other' – just as he was when Sue accidentally lent on his muffins and squashed his handiwork with her elbow. But Deborah was mortified. Sue called it 'the most incredible case of baking espionage I've ever seen'. Within minutes of it being shown, #PoorHoward was a worldwide trending topic on Twitter. Deborah was sent home, and summed up her weekend: 'It started with the wrong custard and ended up as a cascade of misery.'

'They asked Deborah to explain what had happened and to come and apologize, and they reshot that quite a few times, her apologizing, to the point where you think, "Please, stop apologizing, it's fine!"' Howard recalls now. 'So we sort of knew they were going to make something big out of it. We'd handed it to them on a plate, really.'

One by one, bakers fell by the wayside. Toby Waterworth, Lucy Bellamy and Mark Onley were first out. Ali Imdad got as far as episode five, and certainly made an impression on Mary. 'If you don't keep in touch, I'll kill you,' she told him as she gave him the warmest of hugs.

Robert Smart was out despite making Paul the psychic octopus out of bread, and a blue biscuit Dalek stuck together with edible glue. Then it was Howard and cheery schoolteacher Glenn Cosby. Christine Wallace, who constructed a wonderful Bavarian clock tower out of biscuits, was next, followed by Beca Lyne-Pirkis, whose soldier husband had been taking her practice bakes into the barracks for testing ('They liked them all, so that's not very helpful'). Then there were three young women left standing.

*

The all-female final featuring Frances Quinn, Ruby Tandoh and Kimberley Wilson was a high-standard affair. All three bakers were technically brilliant. Ruby, though, was full of doom (or 'Making an appearance for Team Despair', as one blogger memorably put it). 'I feel on the verge of the baking abyss,' she said. For her biscuit tower, she created a 'dropped ice cream' – a metaphor for Ruby's demeanour if ever there was one. Presenting her blackberry and lemon Bakewell tart to the judges in week five, she said: 'I would like to apologize for my Bakewell tart. It's messy, it's under-baked, the pastry's awful as well. I can tell you that now.' But the smile that broke over her face when told she had actually done well was genuine. That dropped ice cream got a rave review from Paul and Mary. 'I'm pleased they liked my bakes more than I seem to,' she mused afterwards.

She and Frances had chosen the same design for their signature bake – a pastry picnic hamper – and Ruby didn't rate her chances: 'It like wearing the same dress, but the other person is a six foot seven Brazilian supermodel.' Yet, surprising everyone, her bake was the best and elicited the ultimate compliment from Paul: 'It looks like Frances made it.'

Kimberley was one of the show's most accomplished bakers, unflustered and self-assured – qualities, it seemed, that some viewers did not welcome. The reaction had her confused. 'The producer would say "Kimberley, you know a lot about the technical part of this, could you just tell us? Because it's the BBC and it's education and it's useful for the audience to know these bits and bobs." And I was like, "Sure." But then people were saying, "Oh my God Kimberley's lecturing us again."'

Kimberley's pretzels were placed first in the final, but her run of good bakes ended there. Her chicken and pig pie had a soggy bottom, and her wedding cake showstopper may have been delicious – a bottom layer of chocolate fudge cake filled with raspberry cake pops sounded like heaven – but the all-white colour scheme failed to impress Mary. Ruby hadn't fully embraced the wedding cake theme (Ruby: 'Weddings are just an exercise in narcissism.' Sue: 'So if you made a wedding cake it would just say, "This will end badly," "One in two marriages end in divorce"').

The winner was Frances, whose midsummer night's dream cake was a gorgeous confection decorated with confetti, flowers and bees. Throughout the series, Paul had accused her bakes of being style over substance. She had marked herself out as a creative genius in the second episode when, tasked with making breadsticks, she dipped the ends in chocolate to turn them into matchsticks. Not only that, but she presented them in a giant matchbox which she'd found the time to decorate to a ludicrously good standard. In the quarter-final, she hid her carrot cake inside a flowerpot filled with edible soil. For Traybake Week, it wasn't enough for Frances to flavour her millionaire's shortbread with banoffee, she had to stack them and present them as a Jenga game. She made a cake with a secret squirrel in it. Her vegetable canapés were in the shape of actual vegetables: choux pastry tomatoes and cauliflower scones.

'I dreamed it,' she said of her win, 'but I didn't think I ever truly, truly believed it.'

*

But there was one other personal triumph in the tent that year, and viewers didn't know it. Christine Wallace had been a high-flying executive for the fashion group Windsmoor before her world came crashing down. In 2012, a year before she appeared on *Bake Off*, she and her husband went on holiday to northern Cyprus. While there she collapsed from a perforated ulcer and stopped breathing. Her husband saved her with the kiss of life. She was flown back to a hospital in England, and her recovery was slow. 'I lost all my confidence,' she says. 'I'd had quite a high-powered job, I had lots of confidence, but it all went. I couldn't even get in the car and drive to Tesco. I was just scared to death.' Her niece, knowing she had long wanted to apply for *Bake Off*, badgered her to apply, 'and she kept on and on, so in the end I thought, "I'll send off the form and she'll stop ringing me." And then at every stage I kept thinking, it's fine, I won't get any further. Until, in the end, I was one of the bakers.'

149

Driving the seventy miles from her Oxfordshire home to Bristol for the start of filming was the most terrifying thing she could think of, but she did it. She said nothing of her illness: 'I don't think Mary and Paul ever knew, I don't think Mel and Sue ever knew. Because I didn't want it to be *X Factor*-ish, I didn't want it to be: "Oh, poor me."' And with every week that went by, taking on new challenges, she found her old self.

'I often say to my husband how *Bake Off* changed both of our lives completely. The people I've met, the things I've done, I never would have done. It really set me on a new path altogether,' she says. 'It gave me back all my confidence and more. It did truly give me my life back.'

THE FLAVOURS

Dessert Week reinvented the trifle. Not for these bakers a sachet of Bird's custard and some Rowntree's jelly. Instead we had coconut, raspberry and lemon meringue trifle; apple and blackberry crumble trifle; peach, almond and ginger trifle – and Christine's Piña Colada trifle. This fabulous concoction with its pink coconut cream custard, pineapple and rum syrup, and mango jam earned her the star baker title. As we know, adding a bit of booze to your pudding is usually guaranteed to impress Mary.

Things got fancy very fast in series four, with the standard of baking higher than it had ever been before. The showstopper challenge in Dessert Week produced things of delicate beauty: limoncello and blueberry bursts, orange financiers, rose and pistachio macaroons, mini blackberry and chocolate layer cakes, spun-sugar plum fairy cakes (those last ones the work of Frances, who remains the most technically accomplished baker of any series when it comes to decoration).

But if it's a stodgy, old-school suet pudding you're after, this series also came up with the goods. Christine and Kimberley both opted for spotted dick. Christine's came with a kick of stem ginger, but was otherwise pretty traditional ('You can't change it too much because otherwise it's not a spotted dick any more,' she explained to Sue, who agreed: 'Otherwise it's just a ginger dick.'). Kimberley went for a Middle Eastern twist, adding Iranian barberries to a pudding the judges thought was absolutely delicious. Other twists on old favourites included roly-poly puddings with figs or plum jam.

And full marks to Glenn for presenting what could be the first Exeter-Milan culinary mash-up: A Devonshire Panettone.

WHAT IS IT REALLY LIKE TO BAKE IN THAT FAMOUS TENT?

IT'S NERVE-RACKING.

The nerves are definitely there in week one, as the bakers get to grips with the fact they're in a competition, being judged by experts, and it's going to be on telly. 'That first programme, we all cut ourselves because we were so nervous and the knives are really sharp,' remembers Christine Wallace of series four. 'Howard ended up in A&E that day. The first aid person was very busy.'

'You walk into the tent and the lady shows you how to use the ovens and the equipment – it must have been five minutes, tops – and then Mel and Sue come out, Paul and Mary come out, and it all happens so fast that you're minutes into the first bake before you realize that you're actually on it,' says Richard Burr. 'It's like a big avalanche of experiences, and quite overwhelming to start with. None of us had ever been on a set, none of us had ever been surrounded by cameras. You're meeting the *Bake Off* people for the first time and you're quite star struck, and you don't know quite what to make of Paul. All of that stuff is tumbling through you, and at the same time you've got to not make a fool of yourself with your very first bake.'

'What made the nerves kick in was when we were on the Baker Bus – that's what we used to call the little minibus from the hotel to the tent – and we drove up that long drive, and we could see the tent across the lake,' says Beca Lyne-Pirkis. 'We all scrambled over to that side of the bus to see the tent. And as we were ushered into the tent, the crew just gave us a massive round of applause and came up and shook our hands and said, "Congratulations, we've heard lots about you." That helped us relax.'

IT'S TIRING.

Somehow, the contestants have to juggle a day job and family life with up to ten weeks on the show. For some, this can mean working all week while practising at night, travelling to the location hotel on the night before filming, getting up to be on set by 6.30 or 7 a.m. for a full day in the tent – at least twelve hours of filming – then doing it again, before making the journey home.

There is lots of waiting around. After completing their bakes, the bakers head off to be interviewed, have lunch or hang out in the green room, while the team get to work on clearing up. At some point the producers also have to film the 'beauty shots' of the finished bakes. 'They make you stare longingly at your bake,' says Simon Blackwell. 'You just end up glaring at the thing.'

IT'S BUSY.

Watch *Bake Off* and the tent appears to contain the bakers, the judges and the presenters working in quiet harmony. In reality, there is also a production crew and all the accompanying equipment.

How do they manage to film all the contestants cooking at the same time, interviewing them all the way through, without any of the camera crews being spotted in the background? Well, watch series one and you'll find they didn't quite manage it. You can spot cameras and cables in the background, or Mel and Sue rehearsing their pieces to camera. Making it look slick has taken years of practice and some very good editing.

Howard Middleton says he was often asked why the bakers don't put things on the floor at the edge of the tent to cool.

'Until you're in there, you don't realize that there's absolutely no room on the floor. But it's so cleverly done that you don't get producers or camera operators in shot.'

'They're all so pro that they individually move with the grace of a gazelle,' says Stu Henshall of series six. 'But because there are so many of them it is pretty distracting.' For the final judging, when the bakers are sitting on their stools waiting to hear their fate, the whole production crew are ranged down the sides of the tent behind the cameras. 'It kind of feels like a red-carpet moment, but no one's getting their camera out.'

'It does feel different than it looks on TV, if that makes sense,' says Dorret Conway of series six. 'When you watch it on TV it looks like natural daylight and, well, a tent. But when you're there it's artificial light, and the machines are humming, and the whole atmosphere of it is different from the impression you get when you're watching it. So the whole thing was a bit not real, if that makes sense.'

IT'S EXPENSIVE.

The bakers have been practising those signatures and showstoppers at home for weeks on end. Some bakers have no idea what they spent to appear on the show. Kimberley Wilson, finalist in series four, stopped counting when she passed £1,000. Sandy Doherty, who reached the fourth week in series six, knows exactly how much it cost. 'I started with a blank credit card, and when it was over there was £2,500, and *Bake Off* was what I used it for,' she says. 'Some of that might be on a new cake tin, because I wanted a certain shape, or buying freeze-dried raspberries. And maybe there was the odd new shirt in there as well.'

BUT IT'S GREAT.

'I call it baking camp. I was having the best time ever. I was getting to go down to this beautiful house every weekend. It was absolutely exhausting and it was expensive. I was a student and I had work to do and all of that sort of stuff. But it was just an extraordinary life experience. I got to find out how a TV programme was made, to meet these people from all over the country. I spent long hours walking around those lovely gardens and picking wild garlic. I absolutely loved it.' (Kimberley Wilson, series 4)

'It was hard, it was stressful, it was confusing because nothing really worked the way it was supposed to. I would never say it was fun, but it was something I wouldn't have missed for the world.' (Mark Onley, series 4)

'It was the loveliest experience of my life.' (Marie Campbell, series 6)

SERIES 5

BIN-
GATE

THE CONTESTANTS

Chetna Makan,
35, fashion designer from Broadstairs, Kent

Claire Goodwin,
31, speech therapist from Trafford

Diana Beard,
69, WI judge from Alkington, Shropshire

Enwezor Nzegwu,
39, business consultant from Portsmouth

Iain Watters,
31, construction engineer from London (by way of Belfast)

Jordan Cox,
32, IT manager from Nottingham

Kate Henry,
41, furniture
restorer from
Brighton

Luis Troyano,
42, graphic designer
from Poynton,
Cheshire

Martha Collison,
17, student from
Ascot, Berkshire

Nancy
Birtwhistle, 60,
retired practice
manager from
Lincolnshire

Norman Calder,
66, retired
merchant seaman
from Buckie,
Moray

Richard Burr,
38, builder from
London

Series five of *Bake Off* gave Britain a new hero.
His name was Norman.

A retired merchant seaman from Buckie in Scotland and a sprightly sixty-six, Norman Calder was an instant hit with viewers. If the list of hobbies in his official *Bake Off* bio didn't draw you in – caravanning, home brewing, walking Lucy the schnauzer – then this line surely did: 'He describes one of his proudest moments as being when he fell overboard three miles off the Solomon Islands in the South Pacific and swam to shore, only to be picked up by an inter-island cruiser near Papua New Guinea.' By the time he started spelling out 'B.A.K.E.O.F.F.' to Sue in semaphore, we were smitten.

Norman didn't go in for fancy decoration. He didn't go in for fancy anything. To Norman, pesto was an exotic foodstuff and tiramisu was something he'd never made and didn't know how to spell. Spectacles perched on the end of his nose, he wielded his lucky spoon ('It's got all sorts of flavours on it, from curry to rice pudding') and showed off his ingenious inventions – a Swiss-roll stand that looked like a skateboard, a bun tin he'd souped up with dowel rods. He creamed his cake ingredients by hand because he couldn't be bothered to plug the mixer in 'just for that'. He considered having one pint less on Saturday night to prepare for the showstopper challenge. He was cheerily honest about the limitations of his bakes: 'I'm not going to put my head up and say that they are the most fantastical-tasting biscuits you've ever had,' is how he sold one of his creations to the judges. In Pie Week, he stacked three pies on top of one another and called them The Pieful Tower. Stormin' Norman, we salute you.

(Norman has famous fans, too. Mara Wilson, the actress who played Matilda in the Hollywood film of that name, declared to her 300,000 followers on Twitter that she wanted him to be her grandfather. Norman says he was pretty chuffed with that.) Mind you, how close we came to a Norman-free *Bake Off*. He only went to the first audition because it was in a city he'd never visited and he fancied a look around. 'The only reason I went was because we'd never been to Manchester before. And then the second audition was in London; the main reason for going down there was to see my two girls, because they live there. So if we had been to Manchester before and my daughters hadn't lived in London, we probably wouldn't have bothered going.'

Anyway, Norman would like to explain about the pesto. 'I was quite advanced as far as food was concerned. I joined the Merchant Navy when I was seventeen and I was on quite a lot of ships with Indian crew, and we got curry three times a day. This is the days before Big Macs and Burger King and Wimpy and all that. But I never tasted pesto until I was fifty-seven. I was down in London and had gone to see my daughter, who was sharing a house with two other students, and she was a vegetarian of course, and she had a bowl of pasta with pesto in it. I said, well, I'll have a taste of that. And I thought, that's jolly good! That was my first introduction to pesto. So when I said on the show that I thought pesto was quite exotic, I wasn't kidding.'

The fifth series wasn't short on characters. Jordan Cox happily described himself as the 'nerdy baker' of the group, devising weird and

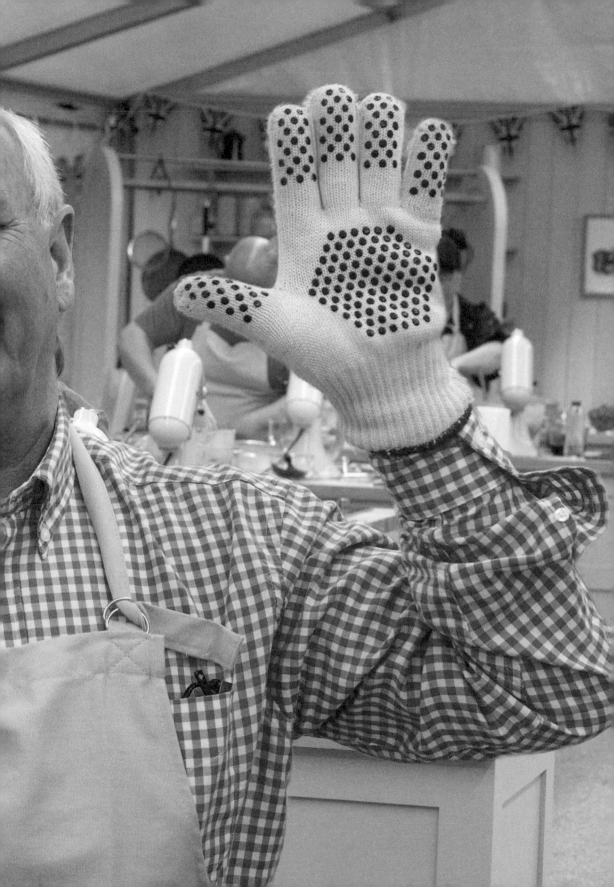

wonderful bakes at home in between playing Dungeons and Dragons and spinning his own wool. His Swiss roll imprinted with giant strawberries was a thing of wonder, made while he sang to himself: 'It's only a cake, it's only a cake, keep telling myself, it's only a cake. . .' And there were some of the most popular contestants the show ever had. They included Richard Burr, a builder from north London who prepared his bakes with that pencil behind his ear as if providing a quote for a loft conversion. (Richard's pre-filming appointment with the *Bake Off* psychologist: 'We chatted about me for five minutes and for the rest of the time we talked about the extension she was having built. I like to feel I add value wherever I go. . .')

Martha was so self-possessed – not to mention bloody brilliant at baking – that it was easy to forget she wasn't yet old enough to vote. Her bakes were full of imagination ('Think Christmas crossed with Chinese New Year, in a bread') and she made it through to the quarter-finals before being eliminated. With an encouraging hug, Sue told her: 'You are seventeen and you are so brilliant and you are going to rule the world, my darling. You rock.' Martha said she had loved every minute, and had discovered how much baking meant to her. 'Obviously I've always cared about it, but I never thought I'd care about it to the point where I'd cry over an éclair.'

*

'The move to BBC1 was carefully managed, but the brief stayed the same – Love weren't asked to look for any more drama or asked by the BBC to do anything differently. There was certainly no unspoken desire to look for the headlines that followed with a very strange situation that saw Diana Beard picked up by the press as someone to sell papers,' an inside source revealed.

At sixty-nine, Diana was the oldest contestant to date. She began the competition as an unassuming Women's Institute stalwart from rural Shropshire. But, to her horror, she soon found herself at the centre of *Bake Off*'s biggest scandal.

She was accused of sabotaging Iain Watters's Baked Alaska by taking it out of the freezer on the hottest day of the year. Iain threw the dessert in the bin and stormed out of the tent, before returning to present Paul and Mary with. . . the bin. Paul was incredulous. Mary gave her best 'I'm not angry, just disappointed' face. Iain was out, and the episode was swiftly dubbed Bingate.

The fallout was immediate. Twitter went into overdrive. *The Sun* front page dubbed it 'Baking Bad' (a play on the drugs drama *Breaking Bad*), the *Guardian* devoted its entire page three to the fallout, and Iain was invited onto *Newsnight* to be interviewed by an apron-wearing Kirsty Wark. Proving that the British public can get irrationally annoyed about pretty much anything, more than 800 viewers took the time to contact the BBC and complain that Iain had been dismissed while Diana lived to fight another day. Many viewers saw her as the villain of the piece.

Diana was distraught. 'Why would I want to sabotage Iain's Baked Alaska?' she said in a tearful interview with her local radio station, claiming that 'the knives were out' for her.

Sue Perkins dismissed it as 'a non-event in the tent' and spoke for reasonable people when she tweeted: 'All getting a little inflamed for my liking. This is a show about CAKES. Please, let's save the ire for the real stuff.'

Things got more complicated when Bingate turned out to be Diana's last appearance on *Bake Off*. It was an unhappy coincidence – the episodes were filmed months before being shown on TV, and it turned out Diana had been unlucky enough to suffer a fainting spell during a dinner with fellow contestants, banging her head and spending the night in A&E with concussion. She left the show on medical advice. But the timing of that announcement, the day after the Baked Alaska fiasco was broadcast, heaped more bad publicity on Diana's shoulders. It all became so fraught that her GP stepped forward to defend her honour in a letter to the *Daily Telegraph*.

No one who worked on the show could quite believe the attention this innocent act had caused. Diana did not take out the ice-cream in malice – as shown by her reaction on the show. It was only out of the freezer for a minute. A Love executive now concedes that: 'In hindsight if that had been made clear in the voiceover, then perhaps there would have been more context for the audience'. At the time of filming, the team were convinced the audience would focus more on the cake being in the bin, rather than on the fact that Diana had mistakenly removed it from the freezer. As one crew member who was there at the time said: 'In all the years of doing the show, there had never been a cake filmed in a bin. We were convinced the press would go crazy for it, but it became the only thing they didn't pick up on!'

Bake Off was now huge. Where once members of the public were allowed to mill around outside the tent and the bakers had to queue for public loos, by 2015 the set had on-site security so lurking paparazzi could not harass them. It was against this background that Diana found herself in the eye of a media storm.

*

Diana entered the show at the urging of her nephews. 'They said one afternoon, "Auntie D, we're going to put you on *Bake Off*." I said, "Are you really, lads? Don't you think I'm a bit long in the tooth?" And they said no, not at all. So that's how it started.'

Like every other baker who landed a place in the programme, Diana sent in her application thinking she had little chance of succeeding and had filled it out in a jokey way. Her answer to the question, 'What do you aspire to?' was, 'Well, to live another ten years would be quite good.' When she heard she was down to the final audition, she had 'collywobbles'. 'But then there's something that kicks in and you think, heck, I can do this. Why can't I do it? Here you are, trundling into semi-retirement, and you think: this is for me. There was something in me that said, "oh, go for it."'

The first Friday night when the bakers all met in a hotel on the eve of filming was great fun. 'It was such an eclectic mix of people, an amazing mix, and we really did get on. We were a good gang.'

And Diana was enjoying herself until Dessert Week. This is how she remembers it: 'It was a very hot day and all the rest of it, and as a group we made a deputation to the production team about why

there weren't enough freezers. The freezers that were provided, half freezers in a domestic fridge, were not up to the job.' (Though there were extra chest freezers to try to help with the heat.)

Diana continues: 'But you do what you can. It was pretty tense, really. And so we all produced something and all our ice creams were running away – Iain's wasn't the only one. Yes, I did take [his] out of the freezer that had been apportioned to Nancy, Chetna and myself. Believe it or not, I know he was only on the other side of the tent, but you're too busy doing your own thing to notice what someone else is doing. And then there was this gasp, and people saying that he'd put it in the bin.

'We all said, oh well, one of us can go home, we're not really fussed. It was that type of day, really. I was sad that Iain had thrown his in the bin because if he'd just produced something for the judges. . . But that was the end of that week. And I was so relieved that I got to Pastry Week.'

Sadly, she didn't make it that far. The following week, during dinner with the other bakers, she fainted in the middle of the restaurant and banged her head. She woke up in an ambulance, and was kept in hospital overnight with concussion. She still believed she would return to the show. 'Next morning, when I cleaned my teeth, I thought, oh, I can't taste that. A couple of days later I suddenly thought, I can't taste a damn thing. I had severed my olfactory nerve, and I've not been able to taste or smell since. And it won't come back. Not a nice experience.'

Three months later, the Baked Alaska episode was aired. Diana was dismayed at the way the viewers reacted to the incident. The media onslaught was brutal. 'It was Iain who told me it was coming. He'd done An Extra Slice and they'd shown him the episode. He rang me and said, "Diana, the knives are out, you're in for a rough ride." And the programme had not finished before the press were onto me. The landline was going, our mobiles were going. And my husband, bless him, said, "Look, the only thing we have left is silence. You cannot cope with this." And that's what we did – we didn't give any interviews, and that has been the way I've got over it, really. I'm not on social media but my daughters are and it really upset me, what people were saying about me.

'What has kept me sane in a certain way is that I've lived in this area all my life and everyone, but everyone, has been supportive. So if I hadn't been on *Bake Off* and that hadn't happened, I wouldn't have known how people felt about me. It was very heartening.'

Iain was mortified by the attention. In his *Newsnight* appearance, preserved on YouTube, he has the bemused air of a man caught in a surreal dream: an amateur baker being interviewed on one of Britain's top current affairs programme, wearing an apron and standing next to a courgette cake. 'It's gone nuts today,' he said. The pressure in the tent had obviously got the better of him, and he felt a bit silly about his behaviour: 'It was just the heat of the moment.'

How do the programme-makers look back on that episode? As was standard practice, the episode had been viewed prior to broadcast by both Love and the BBC. 'No one could have predicted what happened. However, you always look to learn from what has happened. In retrospect, if there's one thing we could have done differently, it would have been to add a line of commentary clarifying that it was only out [of the freezer] for about 50 seconds. That, we hold our hands up to. But nothing is ever perfect,' a Love insider said. 'But that didn't change the outcome. We filmed exactly what happened. Our basic ethos is: will this person at the end feel better than when they went in? And it's really upsetting that Diana hasn't had that experience. We're not in the business of upsetting people.'

There are no hard feelings between Iain and Diana. Far from it. All the bakers were invited to Iain's wedding in 2016 and he had – what else? – a Baked Alaska wedding cake. It was a lovely postscript to an unhappy time. 'They tried to whip up much more of a feud between us than there ever was,' concludes Diana. 'I think Iain and I will be the ones remembered, won't we? Oh dear, dear, dear.'

*

Luckily, we remember series five for plenty of other things. The camaraderie between the contestants is there for all to see. They remain the closest group from any year, regularly meeting up for dinner and chatting on WhatsApp. 'It was a really warm feeling. We were all meant to be in competition against each other, but what we actually found was that the shared experience brings people together,' says Richard. 'Baking has nothing negative about it. You never bake angry. Baking is just a nice thing to do, and nice people gravitate towards it. And it's not like there's a cash prize, so no one was saying, "Ooh, I need the money, so it's a dog-eat-dog world." We were all there to crack on and do it. And it was lovely.'

Richard loved the *Bake Off* experience from beginning to end, and is one of its most cheerful ambassadors. 'As much as every now and again you were up through the night baking, it was just the most wonderful, positive experience.'

Do you know what isn't a positive experience, though? Admitting to Mary Berry that you've used some shop-bought fondant.

Enwezor Nzegwu's Space Adventure Moon Scene looked impressive enough, but Mary had a question. 'Did you make the fondant?' The answer came back: 'No, I didn't.' Cue a stare so cold it could have frozen Iain's ice cream in three seconds. ('This Is The Death Stare Mary Berry Gives If You Really Disappoint Her' was the title of the resulting Buzzfeed coverage).

Three years on, Enwezor remains defiant. 'No one makes their own fondant icing! It's such a waste of time. People had used shop-bought in other episodes and no one came down on them. It just so happened that Mary asked a question and it became a story, particularly as I went out that week. Shopbought fondant is good because it saves you time on something that is basically sugar paste. It's not exactly a skill.'

That look, though. 'The Mary Berry stare,' he shudders. 'It went on so long I think she forgot she was staring at me. Even Paul was getting a bit nervous.'

Meanwhile Norman was having a whale of a time. 'Oh, it was great, great fun. When you get to my age – I'm knocking on a bit now – there's not a lot gets you. I'm certainly not the best baker, that's for sure. How I made it through to week five I'll never know. By that time, you see, I was getting a bit confident. I thought, well, they've had me for four weeks and they haven't seen through me yet, I'll keep going! But despite me turning out a magnificent Pieful Tower, they still decided to send me home. I was shocked. Looking back, I wish I'd tried a bit harder. Paul said I was getting too safe. I hadn't gone too exotic or fandouche.' (Norman has a vocabulary all of his own. In the Christmas special he made 'whisky-flavoured shortbread dingdangs'.)

And it turns out Norman could have averted Bingate, if only Iain had asked him. 'The sad thing was, if he'd spoken to me, I had extra ice cream. I made a big batch and had more than I needed. I sat down and ate a bowl of ice cream at one stage. And it was really good.'

*

The final of series five was between Richard, who had been star baker a record five times; Nancy, the cool as a cucumber 'queen of consistency'; and Luis, the creative genius who had produced some truly stunning bakes, not least a Black Forest cherry tree with a cinnamon trunk.

Luis had also got on Mary's good side by plying her with booze. There is a running joke that Mary likes a drink, and Luis's mudslide and mojito cocktail doughnuts were a hit. 'What you've got there is a coffee bomb with alcohol in it,' sniffed Paul. 'Well, I must say I think this one's absolutely delicious!' grinned Mary, who looked decidedly merry after one slug.

Rain battered the outside of the tent, and maybe that was an omen that the ever-sunny Richard was going to have a shocker. It had looked like his title to lose. But in the Viennoiserie challenge his pain au lait buns, chosen because they reminded him of childhood holidays in France and were the first thing he ate that really got him into baking, were deemed too simple by Paul. In the technical challenge, he literally over-egged the pudding and had to start again. His mini tartes au citron turned into scrambled egg. Luis was a bundle of nerves and failed to deliver, or to impress Paul with his pairing of raspberries and cream cheese. Nancy moved into pole position. 'I feel set up for tomorrow. I feel I could go in now and do it,' she said, as they approached the final challenge.

The brief was to come up with something 'spectacular, enormous and elaborate' and Nancy delivered: the Moulin Rouge, consisting of a cake base, ginger and orange biscuit windmill, mini shortbread decorations and red-dyed caramel sails – that actually turned. At one point a sail fell off, and we saw Nancy quickly repair it and take her bake up to be judged. What we didn't see was that she had

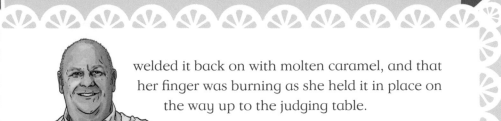

welded it back on with molten caramel, and that her finger was burning as she held it in place on the way up to the judging table.

There was genuine joy from the assembled bakers when Nancy was announced as the winner. 'Without doubt, hand on heart, the right person won,' Luis said. Nancy declared herself 'absolutely overwhelmed and pretty speechless and a bit emotional. Who could believe it, that I could win it?'

And Paul, who she had jokingly referred to as 'the male judge', praised her as a brilliant baker. 'The male judge said, "Have I got a name now?"' Nancy laughed. 'And I said yeah, it's Paul, and I've been secretly in love with you all the time. I had to call you the male judge to be able to control myself.'

THE FLAVOURS

Nobody now remembers what Iain planned to put in his Baked Alaska – the recipe was rather overtaken by events – but they were written down for posterity: chocolate, black sesame seed and coffee caramel. Whether that was a winning combination, we shall never know, but it was probably the most ambitious combination. The others went for more traditional fruit flavours: raspberry ripple, summer pudding, cherry bakewell and Norman's Baked Alaska with Strawberry Surprise. The surprise? It contained strawberries. His Zulu Boats at Dawn in Biscuit Week, disappointingly, did not feature an iced recreation of

Michael Caine's face, but were plain biscuits cut into the shape of boats.

The savoury parcels in Pastry Week contained nothing to scare the horses and all looked delicious: crispy lentil kachori, spinach and paneer samosas, Spanish empanadas, mini beef Wellington, spicy duck and minted lamb pasties. By and large in this series, the bakers kept things relatively simple. They also introduced regional recipes: Nancy's Lincolnshire plum braid was her version of a classic tea loaf said to feature in Royal Family afternoon teas, while Luis conjured up Seventies school dinners with a Manchester tart – shortcrust pastry filled with jam and custard, topped with coconut and a Maraschino cherry.

The self-saucing pudding might sound like a description of Barbara Windsor in her *Carry On* days, but for most of the bakers it meant a dessert with a molten middle: chocolate and salted caramel for Kate Henry, Black Forest chocolate fondant for Richard. This was the series when technical bakes started getting serious: who had previously heard of a prinsesstorta (a Swedish layer cake covered with green marzipan), a kouign-amann (a crusty Breton cake), a povitica (a sweet nut roll), a Schichttorte (a twenty-layer German creation cooked under the grill) or a dobos torte (a Hungarian sponge cake layered with chocolate buttercream)? Imagine the relief to make it to the final and find the technical was a Victoria sandwich cake and some scones.

BEST BAKES

Frances Quinn's secret squirrel cake
(series 4): everything Frances made was clever (apart from that collapsing biscuit tower), but this was something special: a marble cake tree trunk with a chocolate and hazelnut squirrel hidden inside, hazelnut ganache and buttercream tree bark, coconut acorns and chocolate twigs.

Nadiya Hussain's fizzy pop cheesecake
(series 7): a gravity-defying creation featuring a drinks can pouring Italian meringue 'fizz' onto a tier of cakes.

Howard Middleton's Black Forest revisited
(series 4): a three-tiered marvel featuring a biscuit squirrel, chocolate shard trees and a bear called Paul. Mary pronounced it 'a masterpiece'.

Candice Brown's pub
(series 7): Candice recreated her family's pub out of gingerbread, right down to the pool table, the punters, the dog and the telly on the wall.

Rob Smart's Dalek
(series 4): yes, it was a slightly unappetizing shade of blue. Yes, Paul said it only tasted 'OK'. But Mary said: 'Well, it definitely looks like a Dalek,' and that's all the praise you need when you've just made a Dalek out of biscuits.

Luis Troyano's mill town
(series 5): inspired by the history of his home town of Poynton, Luis recreated a local colliery sign out of chocolate and decorated it with tiny choux buns.

Paul Jagger's lion bread

(series 6): the bake to end all bakes, surely? Paul (the other one) declared it 'one of the best things I've seen in bread, ever' and it set Twitter alight. But he still didn't make star baker.

David Chamber's Black Forest floor

(series 1): dark and white chocolate mushrooms, milk chocolate leaves and fallen fruit looked impressive. Although there was something eerie about the sight of his clingfilmed chocolate mushrooms hanging in the fridge like bodies in an abattoir.

Ian Cumming's working well

(series 6): this feat of engineering had a tiny bucket that went up and down, picking up scoops of melted white chocolate. Until Paul broke the handle off.

Victoria Chester's blackbirds in a pie

(series 3): nurseryrhyme inspired, this Sing a Song of Sixpence cake had three birds bursting out of a 'cake' pie.

James Morton's gingerbread barn

(series 3): technically this was a disaster, because the roof and the walls fell off before judging. But in an inspired switcheroo, James draped some cobwebs through the rafters and rechristened it a ruined barn.

SERIES 6
NADIYA

THE CONTESTANTS

Alvin Magallanes,
37, nurse from
Bracknell, Berkshire

Dorret Conway,
53, accountant
from Lancashire

Flora Shedden,
19, art gallery
assistant (and
student) from
Dunkeld, Scotland

Ian Cumming,
41, photographer
from Cambridgeshire

Marie Campbell,
66, retired, from
Perthshire

Mat Riley,
37, fire fighter from
London

Nadiya Hussain,
30, mum from
Luton, Bedfordshire

Paul Jagger,
49, prison governor
from Swansea

Sandy Docherty,
49, child welfare
officer from Yeadon,
West Yorkshire

Stu Henshall,
35, musician from
Guildford

Tamal Ray,
29, a trainee
anaesthetist from
Manchester

Ugnė Bubnaitytė,
32, PA from
Woodford, Essex

The feel-good factor was strong for series six. 'When we were in the tent on the first day waiting for filming, Mel and Sue came in and Mel said, "Oh, wow, there's a really nice atmosphere in the tent – a good energy,"' recalls Dorret. The group bonded instantly.

It was probably the most eclectic line-up yet in terms of occupations – a tattooed rock musician, a female bodybuilder with a passion for healthy baking and a photographer to the Dalai Lama with a recipe for roadkill pie (Ian takes the cake here for best bio). Yet the inclusion of one young woman in a headscarf started a national conversation. By the end of the series, Nadiya Hussain would be one of the most-talked about women in Britain.

Nadiya was a thirty-year-old mother of three from Luton who was persuaded to apply for *Bake Off* by her husband. At the start of the show she was witty and engaging and winningly direct, but noticeably lacking in self-confidence. And that wasn't surprising, because it was the first time she had ever done anything for herself. After school, she had turned down a place to read psychology at King's College, London, because her parents didn't want her to go. She accepted an arranged marriage at nineteen to a man she didn't know – their wedding day was only the second time they had ever met – and spent the next decade as a stay-at-home mum. Wearing Muslim dress made her a target (on her appearance on *Desert Island Discs* she spoke of expecting 'to be shoved or pushed or verbally abused'). She suffered panic attacks, and was too scared to go on public transport in case people tutted at her if she struggled to collapse the buggy. She never went anywhere without her children because she felt they were her identity.

But Nadiya blossomed before our eyes. As each week went by, and as each bake turned out beautifully, she gained confidence. She was forthright and funny. 'I'd sooner have another baby, I really would,' she said when discussing the stress involved in making a soufflé. She soon gained a cult following, largely thanks to the faces she pulled in every episode. They even got their own Tumblr, The Many Faces of Nadiya. Oh, and she had great eyebrows.

Her baking prowess was all the more impressive because she had not learned at her mother's knee, as so many of the other contestants. Desserts are not a feature of Bangladeshi cuisine, and her parents' home had an oven 'only because it came attached to the cooker' – her mum used it as a store cupboard for pans.

'I remember when I first met her. She was super shy, a bit of a wallflower,' remembers Stu Henshall. 'And she just turned into this awesome, awesome entity. She's such a lovely woman. I've got nothing but good stuff to say about her.'

But the inclusion of Nadiya, who was joined in the final by Tamal and Ian, proved controversial. Ally Ross, *The Sun*'s TV critic wrote in a much-pilloried column that Ian was never going to make the final two because he wasn't a Muslim mum or a 'gay Asian NHS worker'.

Ian found the whole argument ludicrous. 'It was interesting, some of the press that we had. The BBC was accused of being overly

politically correct or some rubbish. And I think it was funny how I slightly threw some of the opinions, because you had a Muslim woman, a gay Asian doctor. . . and then me, a middle-aged, white guy with a wife and two kids.'

In fact, the series wasn't any more racially diverse than any that had gone before it. Perhaps it was the fact that Nadiya was so visibly Muslim that brought the line-up into sharp relief. Because when was the last time you saw a woman proudly wearing a hijab on national television, outside news broadcasts?

'Before Nadiya's year, every single winner of the *Bake Off* had been white and no one had said, "Oh, look!" But as soon as a person of colour gets into the final it's: "Oh, it must be because they're a person of colour. That wound me up a little bit," says Ali Imdad. 'Nadiya herself said that being a Muslim was just one facet of her – she's British, she's a mum, she's so many things, but she's never seen as a spokesperson for being British or being a mother, she's seen as a spokesperson for being Muslim.

'And people criticized the *Bake Off* for its diverse casting, but it wouldn't really be representative if we had twelve middle-class white people in the baking tent, even if they were the best in the country. We don't watch because they're brilliant at baking, we watch because we can relate to these people.'

Diversity is part of the show's appeal. 'Reality shows like *Big Brother* capture a minority. *Bake Off* is a TV phenomenon because it captures Britain,' says Mark Borkowski, a PR veteran who has worked on countless television shows. 'Crucially, it represents your Britain. No matter what side of the Brexit debate you sat on, there was something for you to love. If you are middle class or Middle England, if you love *Last Night of the Proms*, if you believe the EU has outlawed bendy bananas – then that bunting-draped tent is your idea of heaven. If you love Britain for its multiculturalism, its dry sense of humour, its capacity to throw a group of complete strangers together and see them bond over a love of flaky pastry – then the programme is for you too.'

Sue may have been joking in her autobiography when she wrote that 'sometimes, when the sound is down, the show can look a little like a UKIP recruitment video, with its jingoistic imagery, bunting and green and pleasant landscape', but she does nail the kitschy, over-the-top Britishness of the whole thing: the Union Jacks, the rolling lawns, the rain drumming down on the marquee. Yet the genius of *Bake Off* is that it fills this fantasy land with a true cross-section of modern Britain: black and white, gay and straight, students and pensioners, regional vowels and cut-glass accents. It is the most quintessentially English show imaginable, and its most popular winner is a Muslim woman in a hijab.

Howard puts it perfectly: 'It's that wonderful marriage of what looks like an idyllic, chocolate box kind of England, and that idea of people coming together, of integration and diversity, which I think is much more the heart of Britishness.'

William Sitwell, the food critic and *Waitrose Magazine* editor says: 'For all we say about Britain being an increasingly enclosed community, that's complete nonsense. Actually, people are very open to listening to people of different class and colour. So it has an exquisite mix of contestants.'

According to Love, confounding preconceptions is in the programme's DNA. '*Bake Off* looks like this conservative place – British, bunting, blah blah blah,' says one executive. 'You could almost say it looks like Brexit. But it's a place which is actually quite radical. It's actually really progressive.'

The thorny issue of class did rear its head in series six, when Flora Shedden suffered a bit of posh-bashing. The student and art gallery assistant was pilloried after admitting she didn't know how to work an electric oven because 'we have an Aga at home'. She also dropped into conversation that at home she had 'over 100 cookbooks. . . most of them in French' and revealed that she learned her biscotti recipe while travelling through Italy. She later pointed out that the Aga dated back to the 1950s. Mind you, a lack of shiny new things is a prime indicator of posh – see also: freezing cold houses and sofa cushions with holes in, where they've been chewed by a Labrador.

If Flora was singled out for her 'poshness', Sandy Docherty believes she was there for people to identify with. 'I think I represented ordinariness,' she muses. 'I work in Bradford. I'm a professional person, but a single working parent from a northern background. If I'd been, I don't know, a part-time GP who was quite affluent and could fund my own baking business, you could imagine people saying, "Ah, yeah, but. . ." I think I came along and there wasn't an "Ah yes, but Sandy can do it because she's got this, she's got that." There was no but.'

And that is the key to *Bake Off*. That anyone can watch it and find someone to identify with, someone to root for.

*

Maybe to truly gauge the Britishness of the show, we need to stand back and look at how the rest of the world views it.

The original *Bake Off* is broadcast around the world, allowing Italians to goggle at Norman's lack of pesto knowledge and Croatians to grade our povitica bread. It is shown in China, bracketed in the same quaint British tradition as *Downton Abbey* and Beatrix Potter. (The Chinese have refused to make a homegrown version, though: Kate Phillips, the executive at BBC Worldwide responsible for selling formats, was informed: 'We don't have formats that make you fat.') In the US, where the later series were aired as *The Great British Baking Show* on PBS and streamed on Netflix, critics have been powerless to resist *Bake Off*'s charms – although they have tried.

'Unlike trash-talking US reality show competitors, the baketestants seem to genuinely respect each other. . . And they all display a character trait missing from most TV competitions: humility,' wrote Marc Silver in the *Washington Post* in July 2016. 'The tent is an island of good manners in an uncertain world.'

In *The New York Times Magazine*, Tom Whyman suggested that *Bake Off* 'is the key to understanding today's Britain', while the *New York Daily News* was suspicious of the weather: 'For the first round, the sun shines brightly into the tent, which may lead weather buffs to ask who stole Britain and replaced it with this imposter.'

Buzzfeed helpfully compiled 'The Clueless American's Guide to *The Great British Bake Off*', in which the author explained that a 'biscuit' is a cookie, 'hundreds and thousands' are sprinkles, a 'bap' is a roll (but 'also has a sexual connotation: breasts'), a 'pud' is a dessert, and 'scone' rhymes with 'gone', although there are millions of Brits who would beg to differ on that last point.

Take the Great and the British out of the title, and you have yourself an international hit to rival *Strictly Come Dancing*. The titles and music are used universally, the competition is run along the same lines, but all have their particular quirks. In one episode of the German show, *The Big Bake*, contestants faced a Bachelor Party Challenge with cakes featuring bondage gear, breasts and a bare bottom (as one BBC executive memorably put it: 'Mary would have had a sh*t-fit if she'd seen it.'). It also reportedly featured a cake flavoured with gherkins, which sounds worryingly like that episode of *Friends* were Rachel gets her cookbook pages stuck together and accidentally puts meat in the trifle.

In France, where it is known as *The Master Pastry Chef*, and things are taken very seriously, each episode lasts nearly two hours and there are cameras inside the ovens to watch the bakes rise (or not). In Norway, the winner gets a new kitchen. In Ireland, the presenter is Anna Nolan, a former nun who appeared in the very first series of *Big Brother*. The Israelis compete in couples. The Danes have the eliminated bakers jumping into a freezing lake. In Turkey, where the show airs five days a week, the bakers opened one episode by dancing at their work stations while waving tea towels. Yes, you read that right. If only this had happened with Norman.

Two US versions of *Bake Off* have been launched. Paul hosted *The American Baking Competition* on CBS in 2013, but that was more notable for his much-regretted affair with fellow judge Marcela Valladolid than it was for decent ratings. Although it stuck closely to the *Bake Off* format, the bakes were as American as they come: peach cobbler, sweet potato pie, 'slap-yo-mama chocolate fudge cookies', a lot of things involving peanut butter. But the innocence of the original was sullied by the $250,000 cash prize, and the stars'n'stripes bunting lacked the twee charms of the British equivalent. It was cancelled after one series.

In 2015, they tried again, this time engaging Mary Berry to judge *The Great American Baking Show* on ABC. A second series was ordered in 2016, but the show has yet to become the success story of its UK counterpart. It seems the US can't quite translate the *Bake Off* formula. Never was this so evident than in a *Saturday Night Live* skit in which the cast tried – and failed – to send up the show. It featured the British actress Emily Blunt somehow doing a bad British accent, and a 'baker' with an even worse accent saying: 'I'm so nervous I'm shakin' in me wellies.' Best to draw a veil over that.

Kate Phillips tried to pin down the appeal of the *Bake Off* format when she gave a talk at the Edinburgh Television Festival. 'For a format to work, so many stars have to align. You have to have the talent, the production, the format, and this is something where everything just came together. People are crying over cakes! It's brilliant. What you want is for people watching not to realize it's come from another country, but to feel it's their own.'

*

Series six got off to a tearful start. Poor Dorret's Black Forest gateau suffered a catastrophic slump. Sue swooped in. 'It's just a cake,' she said reassuringly. 'It's not just a cake,' wept Dorret. Sue was insistent: 'It's just a cake.' Even now, Dorret shudders at the memory. 'Oh, it was horrible. It felt like public humiliation. But whenever people remember it, even people I don't know, they're really sympathetic. They totally understand how I felt and they empathize. It's quite amazing to me how supportive and how nice people were, even on Twitter. And the next week they said, "Yay, you smashed it."' It was Stu who went home in the first week, after his marriage of beetroot and Black Forest gateau failed to impress Paul and Mary.

In Bread Week, Dorret decided to recreate Tracey Emin's unmade bed. This was ambitious and perhaps a little unappetizing, given that the original artwork consisted of Tracey's stained bedsheets, dirty knickers and an overflowing ashtray. Hey ho.

This was also the year that Ugnė bravely attempted to introduce the concept of healthy baking to a show in which the constituent parts are sugar, butter and more sugar. The expressions on the judges' faces when she explained that she was baking with quinoa flour were a picture: strained politeness from Mary, pain from Paul.

Ugnė wonders now if she'd have gone further in the competition without the healthy stuff, 'but it was my choice and what I believe in. Healthier bakes are my passion. It comes from the heart. It was painful when they didn't accept what I loved so much. But I just wanted to show them who I am. Everybody has different taste palates. I can't blame them for that.' Despite that disappointment, she loved her time on the show and would do it all again. 'When you arrive in the minibus on the first day you see these three spikes sticking out of the rooftop of the tent and you think, "Oh my God, it's real!" The memories are wonderful. Was is stressful? It was stressful fun, which I wouldn't change for the world.'

The bakes in Victorian Week were properly off the wall. Let's move quickly past Ian's bubbling pot full of pigs' trotters (he was making his own gelatine for a roadkill pie) and get to the tennis cake. This turned out to be a cake with an edible tennis court on the top. Why? Good question. But it was invented for Queen Victoria in the 1890s. And had pineapple in it. Not only did Mat somehow produce a fluorescent green version that resembled alien goo, but he put his icing in the oven. 'People bring it up still: "Are you the bloke who baked his icing?" Yeah. "Why did you do that?" I'm not really sure. . .' Paul's verdict was damning: 'This looks like a tennis court from Hades.'

In fact the bakes, by this stage in the show, had become so elaborate that if you were able to recreate these at home – well, you were good enough to be a contestant on *Bake Off*. While it is entertaining to watch amazing bakes being created before our eyes, some viewers harked back to the simplicity of the early days. Food historian Dr Annie Gray, who appeared in several series of the show, said: 'I still remember the first series and Mark the bus driver, whose marmalade cake sank in the middle. Of all the people in *Bake Off*, he's the one I remember because his cake was like something I cook at home. That was exactly where most of us watching were at.'

But some bakes just make us bow down in awe. Nothing was more spectacular than Paul's 'King of the Jungle'. It was a lion

bread. A lion. Made out of bread. 'If you say you're going to do a lion,' he said, 'it's got to look like a lion. Not a dog.' It was so good that it earned *Bake Off*'s first – and last – special commendation, after Paul (the other one) praised it as one of the best things he had ever seen made out of bread. Yet the star baker accolade went to Ian, whose black olive and Parmesan bread may have been delicious but was not in the shape of a lion. Twitter was ablaze with outraged fans claiming Paul had been robbed.

＊

The identity of the exiting baker is closely guarded each week. The contestant goes to London on Monday to secretly record an appearance on *An Extra Slice* with Jo Brand. They then have to go about their business until mid-week, when the programme is aired and they can finally tell people their *Bake Off* journey is over.

Except, in the case of Dorret, we all knew she was about to go home. And it was Mary who tipped us off. Appearing on Chris Evans's Radio 2 show, the usually uber-professional Mary dropped a clanger. 'Well, we've already lost two,' Evans said, referring to the contestants who had gone home in previous weeks. 'Wait a minute, we've lost three,' Mary replied. 'We lost Marie last week, Dorret, and on the first week it was our lovely little chap with the hat on.'

Oops.

Was it a slip of the tongue, or what doctors like to call 'a senior moment'? (She had clearly forgotten the name of Stu, aka 'our lovely little chap with the hat on'.) Dorret was unimpressed.

'I was interviewed on radio and I, a complete novice, managed to keep my mouth shut,' she says now. 'Mary has been doing it for six years and she accidentally lets it slip. I was really annoyed. Twitter went mad, it was all everybody was talking about all day. I kept thinking, "How can she be so clued up and let it slip?"' The gaffe got plenty of coverage in the next day's papers. (The *Daily Star* headline put it charmingly: 'Good Evans, Mary, just shut your cake hole!')

By this stage, the national media was publishing *Bake Off* stories on an almost daily basis. Never mind that the BBC only released the contestants' first names – news journalists are nothing if not resourceful, and putting those names together with pictures and details of their home town or profession is usually enough to identify someone. Once the bakers' pictures are made public, newsdesk phones start ringing with 'friends' proffering gossip. And as the series got bigger each year, so the pressure from editors to deliver *Bake Off* stories increased.

In Sandy's case, the press dug up a past relationship. She was shocked when a journalist came to her door.

'I never really thought much about the fame. I wanted *Bake Off* to generate another kind of world for me. I mean, I work in child protection, and for the last ten years of my career I wanted to bake somewhere, to run a community café to support the kids I work with. I went on *Bake Off* with a lot of innocence, not thinking that the press would be interested. Yes, it's fair game, you put yourself out there – I get that. But I thought it would be more about what I wanted to do afterwards, and that was quite naive.'

For some, the attention was quite amusing. When journalists mined Richard Burr's Facebook page for info, they discovered he'd done a degree (he had studied for it part-time, in the evenings, while working in his family building business by day) and had been scuba diving on holiday. This was enough to convince the *Daily Star* he wasn't a real builder, and to draw the rather stretched conclusion that he was 'as working class as Old Etonian David Cameron'. It didn't end there. Richard says: 'In the lead-up to the final, a bunch of hacks were coming along and speaking to all the local building suppliers. There was one journalist who found my address and literally must have gone to every building supplier within a two-mile radius. Luckily, we'd paid all our bills. I'm the fourth generation of our business, we get on with all our suppliers, so they weren't able to get any dirt, and I'm quite happy about that. I don't really have any skeletons in my closet. I feel quite sorry for people who have.'

Marie Campbell also found herself targeted in the press: accused of being a professional baker on the sly. In fact, she had done a week-long patisserie course at the Ritz in Paris. . . thirty years earlier.

*

As the final loomed, Nadiya became the subject of political interest. David Cameron, facing a crisis in his party over the EU referendum, nevertheless took time out of the Tory party conference to say he loved *Bake Off* and was backing Nadiya because she was 'cool under pressure'. Not to be outdone, George Osborne claimed his family adored the show so much that they spent every Saturday making a *Bake Off* cake and had recently produced a Spanische Windtorte.

The brief for the final showstopper was to create a British celebration cake. Ian's 'colossal curvy carrot cake' was an ambitious undertaking – five separate cakes of increasing size, arranged on a giant tiered stand – and got the Paul Hollywood seal of approval. Tamal had a novel interpretation of the British theme – and for 'novel', read 'crazed' – which was to make an abandoned Chinese fishing village out of sticky toffee sponge. But Nadiya's was perfect. It was the wedding cake she'd never had, because she had married her husband in Bangladesh, where cake is not a feature of weddings, and decorated it in red, white and blue. It looked stunning. The *Bake Off* crown was hers.

The sheer joy of Nadiya and her family was enough to get the nation, and Mary, welling up. And then there was her speech. 'I'm never going to put boundaries on myself ever again.

I'm never going to say I can't do it. I'm never going to say "maybe". I'm never going to say, "I don't think I can." I can and I will.' It wasn't a message about being Muslim, or wearing a hijab. It was a message that every person watching could relate to.

Since the show, Nadiya's career has skyrocketed. She made a cake for the Queen's ninetieth birthday, admitting she was shaking with nerves before presenting her three-tiered orange drizzle cake, and summing up her excitement afterwards: 'I thought meeting Lenny Henry was going to be the pinnacle of my career!' She wrote a novel (albeit with a little help from a ghostwriter), *The Secret Lives of the Amir Sisters*. She introduced viewers to Bangladesh in a documentary, *The Chronicles of Nadiya*, in which she visited her family village and shared favourite recipes. And a year after her win, she signed a big-money deal to make *The Big Family Showdown* with Zoe Ball. 'I never thought this would happen, but it is. And, I have to admit, I'm going to embrace it,' she said.

The BBC praised her 'refreshingly authentic voice, great warmth and charisma and a natural ability to connect with audiences'. What they didn't say was that the golden handcuffs deal also effectively prevented her from going to Channel 4, where the search for new *Bake Off* presenters was quietly getting under way.

Nadiya's win was watched by over 15 million people, the biggest TV audience of 2015. But if there's one person who could bring you down to earth after such an extraordinary year, it is the Duke of Edinburgh. He was there when Nadiya presented her cake to the Queen at Windsor.

'Prince Philip came over and she introduced me to him. I was like, "Oh my God, that's the Queen introducing me!"' Nadiya said afterwards. 'She said, "This is the young lady who won the *Bake Off*." 'And he said, "Yes, dear, I know who she is. But what flavour is the cake?"'

*

Adjusting to being famous is an odd experience for a bunch of ordinary people whose claim to fame is that they baked on a TV show. In the beginning, at least, you're still doing your day job, yet being approached in the street for autographs and attracting a fevered social media following.

'I went to the Edinburgh Festival in August. I was meeting my sister in this garden and I was followed by a group of people. My sister said, "Who are these people?" And I said, "Oh, they've been following me and asking for an autograph but I knew I was late so I just ran on." I happened to have made my sister some biscotti; I handed her the tin, and she just opened it and started handing all these people biscotti.' (Marie Campbell, series 6)

'It was a funny thing. I had 14,000 people following me on Twitter. I did a quick scan of their ages, most of them were female and young. All about forty years too late, unfortunately! I probably reminded them of their grandfather.' (Norman Calder, series 5)

'We were away on holiday in France when the first episode was on. Life was ticking on as normal there, but then we went back through Calais passport control and a British customs lady handled the passports. With a serious face she looked through them and then said, "Just one more question. . . *Bake Off*?"' (Ian Cumming, series 6)

'When it aired, I was working as a doorman in Newmarket. A police lady ran through traffic, across the High Street, and I thought, Christ, what's going on? Police officers don't usually run through Newmarket. And she said, really official, "You are Simon from *Bake Off*, aren't you?" And then: "Can you sign my book?"' (Simon Blackwell, series 2)

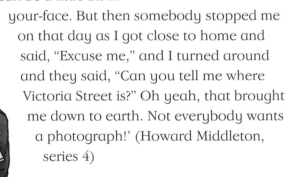

'I remember one day when I was in the centre of Sheffield, I must have got stopped about ten times by people wanting photos and things like that. Which is lovely, but you think, oh gosh, this can be a little bit in-your-face. But then somebody stopped me on that day as I got close to home and said, "Excuse me," and I turned around and they said, "Can you tell me where Victoria Street is?" Oh yeah, that brought me down to earth. Not everybody wants a photograph!' (Howard Middleton, series 4)

THE FLAVOURS

Paul's bread lion was, of course, the most incredible thing ever to be made out of bread in the shape of a jungle animal. But let's not forget the other efforts. Tamal made a breadcycle, with marzipan and cranberry wheels, a fennel and lemon chain, and a basket on the front containing a chai-spiced roll. Flora made a corset, Mat recreated Brighton Pavilion, and Sandy made a basket of. . . bread.

The most alarming-sounding bake of the series was Ian's roadkill pie. He hadn't actually run over the venison, partridge and guinea fowl that went into the filling, but explained that he was inspired by the time he found a squashed hare in the road and took it home for tea.

Pastry Week was all about vol-au-vents, and there were plenty of ideas here to impress the neighbours when you invite them over for Christmas drinks (then curse them for not bringing a bottle but being last to leave after hoovering up the Chablis): Parma ham and asparagus, chicken and coriander, fennel and rosemary pulled pork. Nadiya's fillings got a thumbs-up from the judges: clementine and cod, and Bengali korma. Unfortunately, she royally messed up the timings and had to present the fillings in a bowl next to her pastry. Meanwhile, Mat introduced the concept of gendered vol-au-vents, with a 'His'n'Hers' offering of bacon and egg, and smoked trout with horseradish. They were even good enough to make him that week's star baker.

Vol-au-vent disaster aside, this series belonged to Nadiya, and the list of her creations is mouthwatering: quadruple Black Forest gateau, orange and green cardamom madeira cake, Mexican bread with warm tomato salsa, mango and raspberry

Charlotte russe, and that trio of fizzy pop cheesecakes. Her favourite flavour combination, she says, is chocolate, salted caramel and peanuts, all featured in a tart that saw her through to the semi-final.

ARE THE BAKERS REALLY THE BEST OF FRIENDS ON SET?

Mainly, yes, although as things hot up towards the final, some rivalry does sneak in. Janet Basu, series two veteran, hoots with laughter when told that other bakers insist it's all peace and goodwill to the very end. 'Hahaha. What rose-tinted spectacles some people have! I mean, initially they were lovely, nice people. I was happy to be with them; loads of people I'd never normally have met, so it was really interesting if you like people, which I do. But it would be absolutely untrue – I mean, nice to think, but untrue – to say that by the time we got halfway through, people weren't fiercely competitive. Not everybody, but some people.

'I'm not very competitive. I just couldn't treat it as the end of the world, because I was more surprised than anyone to be on it. For me it was such fun. I really loved it. I was delighted when things went well and not over-upset when things went badly. [But] it was interesting to see, as the numbers dwindled and people were sent home, how people's competitive natures came out. I understand that, though. Whereas I'm quite ancient, some of them were quite young and obviously could see a change of career and lots of potential, so I don't blame them for being competitive. It didn't mean people couldn't smile at each other, but with teeth clenched at times.'

A fellow baker from series two remembers it a bit differently. 'Janet,' they whispered, 'was really competitive.'

And it doesn't end with filming. 'I have met *Bake Off* people from the past and I can see even now that they're competitive with other *Bake Off* people, even after *Bake Off* has finished. It's true, I've seen it with my own eyes!' says Chetna Makan, who had no such problems with her fellow bakers from series five. 'In our year, we genuinely liked each other and whoever needed support we were there to support them.'

There are hints that relations on set weren't always perfect. Series three winner John Whaite said after the show ended: 'There was some backstabbing and snide comments. But it's a competition at the end of the day. What did annoy me was people coming into it saying, "I'm only here for the fun, I don't want to win." Rubbish! You don't enter something like *Bake Off* unless you think you have a chance of winning.'

Paul concurred: 'If they're going to do television, believe me, they're ambitious.'

But stories of bad behaviour are rare. Series five, six and seven, in particular, were a love-in. Stu Henshall says of the first time he met his fellow bakers, at a hotel the night before filming began: 'You kind of feel like you've already won just by being there. It was almost like opening the chocolate wrapper with the golden ticket.'

Sandy Docherty says: 'Baking is not an aggressive sport, is it? So it usually doesn't have cut-throat, aggressive people in it. You've got personalities that are very, very similar in that there's this tranquillity. You've all got this common ground, you've all gone through the same process for the last six months.'

'It's like going along to a convention or a party where everybody has got something in common. And it's very rare to do that out in the real world. You don't tend to stumble across fellow bakers, so it's a real pleasure and a privilege to have that in the group,' says Howard Middleton.

For some groups the bond was instant. 'For anyone to be there, you have to be a pretty big baking enthusiast, so it's like a geekfest of baking. We all talked about baking all the time. It was fun,' says Enwezor Ngwezu of series five. His group chat regularly via Whatsapp and meet up for dinner. And Kimberley Wilson says of series four: 'We have baking days where we all catch up. We'll go to someone's house, lay on the ingredients and have a little bake, then all watch TV and get a takeout.'

And then there was the friendship between Mary, Paul, Mel and Sue.

There is little fraternizing between the bakers and judges. Mary and Paul had as much contact with the contestants as we saw on screen, save the odd bit of small talk outside the tent, in order to maintain a professional distance. They embarked on what the crew jokingly referred to as the 'Royal Tour', visiting each workstation for a short chat about the bakes. But for most of the day, including the duration of the technical challenge, they sat in the green room. Mel made it her mission to get Mary into *Breaking Bad*, and brought along the box-set. It was a family affair: Mel brought along her kids, Mary had family members come to visit (including, for series one, her 104-year-old mother). Beca Lyne-Pirkis remembers Sunday afternoons at Harptree Court: 'I used to play football with Mel's girls when we had downtime. It was nice getting to meet Mary's daughter and the grandkids. It was like normal life – and then the cameras go back on and you have to go back into the Tent of Doom.'

At the end of each night, the bakers go back to their hotel and out for a meal. Some years they have group meals; in other years, particular friendships formed and certain bakers would head out to a restaurant together. Meanwhile, Paul and Mary had their own routine. He shared it on *Desert Island Discs*: 'I drive her everywhere. When we leave the tent and go to the hotel, she always has a cold Chardonnay. I normally have either a Hendricks or a G&T and we sit outside and put the world to rights. Then we have dinner, and after half an hour up she goes to her room and says, "Do you need any ironing doing?"'

SERIES 7

THE
MOVE

THE CONTESTANTS

Andrew Smyth,
25, aerospace
engineer from
County Down

Benjamina Ebuehi, 23, teaching
assistant from south
London

Candice Brown,
31, PE teacher from
Bedfordshire

Jane Beedle,
61, garden designer
from Beckenham,
Kent

Kate Barmby,
37, nurse from
Norfolk

Lee Banfield,
67, pastor from
Bolton

Louise Williams,
46, hairdresser from
Cardiff

Michael Georgiou,
20, student from
north London

Rav Bansal,
28, student support
worker from Erith,
Kent

Selasi
Gbormittah,
30, client services
associate from
London

Tom Gilliford,
26, project manager
from Rochdale

Val Stones,
66, retired
headmistress from
Yeovil, Somerset

David Cameron chose 12 September 2016 as the day to announce he was leaving politics. He stood down as MP for Witney after fifteen years, calling time on a career that had seen him rise to the highest office in the land and trigger the nation's biggest postwar crisis by calling the referendum that would see Britain leave the European Union.

Really, though, who cared? It was also the day the BBC lost *Bake Off*. Dave was shoved off the front pages by the shock news that Channel 4 had poached the show for a reported £75 million. 'Crumbs!' said the *Mail* and the *Mirror*. 'Dough! Beeb Loses *Bake Off*,' yelled the *Daily Star*. 'Desserted,' thundered the *Sun*. As the BBC's political editor Nick Robinson tweeted in the wake of Cameron's announcement: 'Politics is a cruel business. *Bake Off*'s Off will be a bigger story than Dave's Off.' It was probably a bigger story in Cameron's own house, given that his wife, Samantha, had won the *Sport Relief Bake Off* with that terribly chic tray of crab vol-au-vents.

It was not, Love Productions said, about the money. Insiders claimed they moved the show to Channel 4 'with a heavy heart' and tried their best to keep the original talent on board. But it wasn't to be.

Behind the scenes, it emerged, relations between the BBC and Love had been tricky for a while. It dated back to 2014, when the BBC announced a show called Hair that aimed to find the nation's best amateur hairdresser. Love felt that it was virtually identical to their baking show and threatened to sue. It was settled, but it meant the two sides were fighting it out via their lawyers at exactly the same time as they were trying to sign a deal to move the show to BBC1. A year later, a similar conversation took place about another BBC show: *The Big Painting Challenge*. The matter went to mediation, but was not resolved and the relationship was severely soured. Negotiations to renew the *Bake Off* contract had begun in the spring of 2016, and things were not going well. For seasoned media watchers, the clues were there that the future of *Bake Off* lay elsewhere. Charlotte Moore, controller of BBC1, was interviewed at a television event, by chance on the day series seven launched. She was asked if *Bake Off* would be staying at the BBC. Her reply? 'I would never talk about negotiations publicly, but safe to say that *Bake Off*, the first episode is absolutely fantastic, it's at the top of its game, it's really reinventing, we've got a fantastic cast, my focus is absolutely on this series and I can't wait for everybody to enjoy it.' Translation: I'm waffling because it's panic stations back in the office.

Although the BBC increased their financial offer, the two sides had deeper issues that couldn't be resolved.

The show had been originally commissioned as a documentary programme – remember all those history bits in the first series? – and that meant a relatively low budget. Love wanted it reclassified as entertainment, which commanded more money, plus assurances that the BBC were committed to the future of a show that was fast becoming an institution.

The stand-off between the BBC and Love culminated in a meeting at Broadcasting House in September 2016, when it became clear that relations had irretrievably broken down. Within hours, to the astonishment of just about everyone, it was announced that *Bake Off* was leaving the BBC and had a new home on Channel 4.

Channel 4 boss Jay Hunt had snapped up the show because she was anxious that other broadcasters might swoop in or that the BBC might have a last-minute rethink and up their offer. It meant the deal was concluded without a guarantee that the

judges or presenters would remain with the show. Channel 4 hoped that Mel and Sue, who had got their big TV break on Channel 4 with *Light Lunch* all those years earlier, would make the transition too. But they swiftly severed ties in their inimitable way, declaring: 'We are not going with the dough.'

They were followed by Mary, who remained loyal to the BBC and did not enter into direct discussion with Channel 4: 'I avoided being asked. It was suggested what would happen if I did go to Channel 4: what I would get, the advantages. But I didn't ever have a meeting with them. I'd made up my mind. To me, it's an honour to be on the BBC. I was brought up on it,' she told the *Radio Times*. She recalled listening to BBC broadcasts during the Blitz. 'Everybody went silent when it came on. We followed the war all the way with the BBC.'

Only Paul Hollywood decided to stick around.
And who could blame him? *Bake Off* had
made his career, and his loyalties, quite
rightly, lay with the show. But if the
country was divided over Brexit, it was
all of one mind over the departure of
The Great British Bake Off. It was treated
as a national disaster. This calamity
even made the pages of *The New York
Times* and *Washington Post*. Buzzfeed's
Scott Bryan, whose *Bake Off* articles had
been read by an international audience,
says: 'I remember receiving emails from
readers and colleagues who weren't familiar with all the politics
behind it, saying, "What on earth is going on with your country?
You had Brexit and now you're somehow managing to screw
up one of the biggest shows Britain has known?"'

And if the production company had hoped all the opprobrium
would be heaped on the BBC for failing to hang on to the
show, they were disappointed. Although Love felt they had no
alternative, they were accused of putting greed before viewers,
and Paul bore the brunt of it. The same journalist who described
Paul as 'the crumpet-making woman's crumpet' was now
condemning him for jumping ship to Channel 4 'with the
greedy alacrity of a sugar rat up a marzipan drainpipe'.

After three months, Paul broke cover and granted an interview
to *The Times* in which he told how bruising the experience had
been. 'It hit me like an express train,' he said of the criticism.
'I haven't murdered anyone, but I think the Yorkshire Ripper
got less press than I did.'

Losing Mel and Sue 'was like my parents had split up. It broke me in half. I was gutted,' he said. He had not called Mary and asked her to stick with the show because he didn't think it would be fair to influence her decision. Mary was a little more circumspect when asked about Paul once the two had gone their separate ways. 'Paul and I had our differences about what was important to us but he is a brilliant bread-maker and I admired him a lot.'

So who was to blame for the BBC losing *Bake Off*? The corporation points out that it does not have a bottomless pit of money and can't be seen to splash tens of millions of pounds of licence fee money while making cutbacks elsewhere. Love take a very different view. 'What we did, it didn't happen suddenly and it didn't happen just for money,' says a production company insider. 'It was many factors all coming together that finally brought us to the point of breaking. We thought through all the risks, knew we couldn't necessarily take all the talent with us.

'But, you know what? We want *Bake Off* to be here in thirty years' time. So we thought, where's a safer place?'

They found themselves facing an enormous challenge, though: how to recreate the chemistry of the much-loved original line-up?

The producers started to compile a list of potential male and female judges to work alongside Paul. This list went through many revisions and by November there was a shortlist. In January 2017 a week of screen tests took place that were filmed and edited before being sent to Channel 4. One potential judge, in particular, excited the channel – Prue Leith.

Described by Paul Hollywood as 'cookery royalty'. Prue is Cordon Bleu-trained, founder of Leith's School of Food and

Wine, and has a Michelin-starred restaurant under her belt. Like Mary, she has written several cookery books. She is also a veteran of this kind of show after years as a judge on the BBC's *Great British Menu*. The programme-makers describe her judging style as 'constructive honesty'.

Prue was the first name to be announced to the public. It tested the waters: how would fans react to someone replacing their beloved Mary? But the response was positive, and Prue was confirmed as the new judge.

Once the new judge was in place, the search began for the new hosts. The eventual choice was more of a shock. Sandi Toksvig and Noel Fielding? The star of surrealist comedy *The Mighty Boosh* and possibly Britain's only glam rock goth teaming up with Radio 4 stalwart, cerebral quiz show host and all-round good egg, Sandi? Could we imagine them trading banter in the tent with Paul and Prue? Noel acknowledged the weirdness of it all. 'We do all get on, which is odd, as you couldn't have put more unlikely people together,' he said in his first interview about the show.

Sandi was hired first – she had worked with one of the *Bake Off* executives in the past and had been suggested as a good fit, not least because of her gentle warmth that puts contestants at ease. To check that Noel could also interact with humans, Love Productions took him to a garden centre and asked him to chat to members of the public. 'It was a hit and a great indication of how he might be with the bakers,' one member of the team explained. Sandi reassured fans straight away that Noel was the right man for the job, saying: 'He is a huge fan of the show. I'm absolutely confident he will bring the same level of love that I'll bring to it.' According to the team, Sandi and Noel are 'a match made in heaven'.

As the months went by, the public began to forgive Paul. Just a little bit. He readily admitted that for him it was – in part – about the money. 'If you could double your wages by going across the road to a rival, would you?' he asked. Ultimately, though, he made the decision out of loyalty. '*Bake Off* made me. Why would I turn my back on them?' He also insisted that the foursome remain friends, and revealed that Sue had texted him after his big-money move. The message said: 'Lend us a tenner.'

*

The summer of 2016 was dominated by Brexit. The referendum on 23 June resulted in a vote to leave the European Union. The political classes were at war; neighbours, friends and family were pitted against each other. Could *Bake Off* hold the nation together?

The casting for series seven was perfect. There was the heart-throb (Selasi), guaranteed to send Twitter into a weekly frenzy; the eccentric (Val, who did keep-fit exercises at her workstation and talked to her cakes: 'I listen to my cakes. They sing, and they're saying, "Not ready!"'), the sensitive young man with a plaid shirt (Andrew), who planned his bakes on an Excel spreadsheet; and there was Candice, the PE teacher with an A+ lipstick game and perfect baking skills.

There was no great drama – Candice changing her lip colour

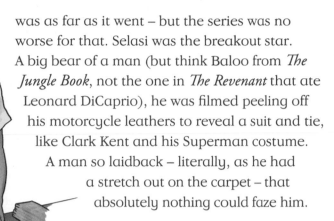

was as far as it went – but the series was no worse for that. Selasi was the breakout star. A big bear of a man (but think Baloo from *The Jungle Book*, not the one in *The Revenant* that ate Leonard DiCaprio), he was filmed peeling off his motorcycle leathers to reveal a suit and tie, like Clark Kent and his Superman costume. A man so laidback – literally, as he had a stretch out on the carpet – that absolutely nothing could faze him.

Forgotten to put a key ingredient in the bake? No idea what a Palmier is? Running out of time to construct some stained-glass windows for the gingerbread church? Not a problem. If you can keep your head when all about you are losing theirs over where to put the jelly disc in a Jaffa cake, you will go a long way in this competition. 'It's your first technical challenge. How can you be so cool?!' marvelled Mel in week one, as Selasi sauntered around the kitchen, tea towel over his shoulder, with the air of a man on the world's most relaxing beach holiday.

That gingerbread challenge was the highlight of the series. Contestants were required to create a three-dimensional gingerbread story representing something important in their life. Oh, and it had to be at least 30 cm high. Candice recreated her parents' pub, complete with a sticky (ginger cake) carpet, bar, dartboard, dog and pool table with lime-green jelly baize. Andrew constructed a thirty-seven-piece punt

along the River Cam. Michael tried to conjure up a childhood trip to Lapland, which turned out more like 'Santa's workshop from hell'. Poor Louise attempted to build the church in which she planned to get married, only for it to collapse in a heap, moments before she was due to present it. 'I'm so sorry for your future husband,' deadpanned Paul as he surveyed the destruction. Louise went out with admirable honesty: 'I came, I tried, I had a disaster. I'm accepting it and going home.'

And Val? Paul and Mary had counselled her in previous weeks about knowing her limitations. Ever the optimist, she decided to create a Yorkshire mining village, a Dutch windmill, the Empire State Building (with the correct number of windows) and the Statue of Liberty, all in one bake. Oh, and her sister Susan. As she was about to carry the thing up to the judging table, Liberty's head fell off. 'Bless her. She gave up,' sighed Val.

Alas, Selasi failed to make it past the semi-final. A nation mourned. Mel and Sue fought over who could give him the longest farewell hug. Paul was bereft at the end of their bromance. Mary said: 'No one's more sad than me to say goodbye to Selasi.' We wouldn't be too sure about that, Mary. And the man himself? Totally fine. Why wouldn't he be? He's Selasi.

It wasn't the last the other bakers saw of him. Selasi hosted a viewing party for fellow bakers every Wednesday that the show was on, posting pictures on social media of his catering: Philly cheesesteak, jerk chicken, griddled octopus, eight-hour slow roasted pork. . . Selasi can do more than bake. The one time he didn't cook, he laid on two dozen pizzas, buckets of champagne and some confetti cannons. And he has been all over the country on his bike, visiting the other bakers.

A record 15.9 million people tuned in to see Candice win the final, the biggest audience since the London 2012 Olympics. She looked genuinely shocked when her name was read out, although her baking had been so consistently great that plenty of people had marked her out as the winner from the very start. 'I never, ever, ever thought I would even get on this and I'm standing here now and they said my name,' she said through tears.

Of course, nobody filming the show knew that it was to be the last series with the team all together. Several months later, when the dust had settled, Mel said: 'There's sadness, of course, because it was seven absolutely brilliant, vintage years of great fun and genuine friendship between the four of us. But we've got to be grown-ups.'

THE FLAVOURS

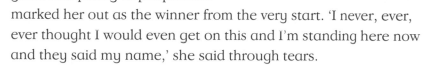

The only proper accompaniment to Yorkshire puddings is gravy. This is one of life's inviolable rules. Unfortunately for purists everywhere, *Bake Off* was running out of signature bake ideas by series seven. Hence 'Batter Week' and the most terrible Yorkshire crime scene since the police drama *Happy Valley*: Rav's Thai Tofu Panang Yorkshires. Bird's eye chillis, Thai shrimp paste, kaffir lime leaves, cubed tofu, fish sauce and a lime garnish were all involved. We must never speak of these again.

By contrast, Val's Yorkshire puds filled with chilli con carne, and Benjamina's onion, brie and bacon creations seemed positively traditional.

Rav was the flavour maverick of series seven. He served his churros with wasabi, put cardamom in his chocolate loaf, and laced his drizzle cake with yuzu. His samosas were filled with white chocolate, hazelnuts, chilli powder and cloves. His mandarin meringue pie was infused with tequila – Andrew claimed it was the nicest thing he had ever tasted.

This year was packed with unusual bakes: Bread Week featured barmbrack – an Irish loaf with sultanas and raisins, often served hot and buttered – and babka, a brioche-style cake served at Easter in some Eastern European countries.

We also had palmiers (puff pastry biscuits sometimes known as 'elephant ears' due to their distinctive shape), dampfnudel (a sweet bun that is steamed, not baked), herb fougasse (Provencal flatbread similar to focaccia), marjolaine (a French gateau of praline and almond and hazelnut meringue, coated in chocolate ganache), Savarin (a variation on rum baba) and jumbles (a feature of Tudor Week, these are little biscuits flavoured with vanilla, aniseed or caraway seed).

Yet it was the humble Jaffa cake that had the bakers really flummoxed. Which way up does the orange jelly disc go? How big should it be? And would anyone really make their own, rather than pop to the corner shop for a packet?

Candice returned to her job as a PE teacher straight after the final, but within weeks of its broadcast she had been snapped up by the agent who represents Paul Hollywood. She quit teaching, and who could blame her? 'This has been such an agonizing decision to make,' she said at the time. 'But since winning the final, I have also been completely bowled over by the amazing opportunities that I have been offered.'

For every baker, life will never be quite the same. No winner can match Nadiya for post-*Bake Off* success. Her life story, her bucketfuls of charm and a face the camera loves proved an irresistible combination. But the others haven't done badly for themselves. Edd Kimber, Jo Wheatley, John Whaite, Frances Quinn, Nancy Birtwhistle, and now Candice – all have turned baking into a career.

In the two weeks after Jo won the second series, she received 'something like 15,000 emails'. Thirteen publishers entered a bidding war for her first book, which topped *The Sunday Times* bestseller list. 'Since then, I think people have ideas of what they want to achieve. They want to be famous, basically,' she says. 'But bear in mind that when our series was on, Edd hadn't brought out his book yet. Nobody had done anything at that point. So I had no preconceptions about achieving anything.'

In more recent years, though, you would need to have lived in a hole in the ground not to know that *Bake Off* can bring fame and fortune. (Although you should be wary of newspapers that say someone is 'tipped to make £1 million'. That's journalist speak for 'This person will probably make a lot of money, but I haven't the foggiest how much, so let's go with a nice round number.')

Inevitably, an increasing number of people who apply for the show have this in mind. It is now pretty much de rigueur for bakers to have gorgeous, professional-looking blogs up and running before they even set foot in the tent. It is the job of the production team to sift through the applicants and weed out those who are secretly professional, and those who are applying for the wrong reasons. Indeed, of the eighty-three bakers to have appeared on the BBC show, eighteen have bagged book deals.

Yet the producers do manage, each year, to turn up a bunch of people who love to bake. And it is that passion which sets it apart from other shows. Nobody goes on *Big Brother* these days because they think it's a fascinating social experiment. It's a rare contestant on *The Apprentice* who wants a job for life with Alan Sugar, rather than ten weeks of free publicity for their dubious business idea. *Bake Off* is different.

Some of the bakers slipped back into their old jobs as nursery workers, midwives, engineers, teachers, credit controllers, accountants, nurses, dentists or doctors. Others manage to juggle a career with forays into the baking world – appearing at food festivals and cake shows, popping up on TV, working with brands, writing recipes and hosting cookery courses. Series three runner-up James Morton managed to qualify as a doctor and produce three books. His blog is a mix of cinnamon bun recipes and lengthy posts about the plight of the NHS. Tamal Ray, series six heart-throb, is now a TV presenter and an anaesthetist, with a book in the works. Being a familiar face does have its uses in the operating theatre. 'If we've got a nervous patient, sometimes our consultants will just bring it up straight away: "Oh, remember him? He was on *Bake Off*," as a thing to distract them.'

Kimberley Wilson combines her work as a psychologist with TV presenting and writing recipes for her blog. 'Some people were immediately like: "I'm getting the hell out of this job, see ya later,"' she says. 'I got a lot of people asking me if I was going to quit psychology now – even psychologists! I was like, guys, I love my job and I just spent ten years training to do it. So I made the decision to try to do a little bit of both.'

Others took the profile gained from appearing on *Bake Off* – and the confidence it gave them in their own abilities – to open baking businesses. Johnny Shepherd entered the very first series because he dreamed of reopening his family bakery. He didn't quite do that, but he did open The Pudding Stop, serving steamed syrup sponge and blackberry and apple crumble to the residents of St Alban's. It hosts regular *Bake Off* screenings. Cathryn Dresser from series three opened a cake shop but sadly it closed within a year. Even having *Bake Off* on your CV doesn't make you immune to tough times on the High Street.

Marie Campbell insists she didn't see *Bake Off* as a means to establish a new career in her sixties, but that's exactly what happened. She is now the proud owner of Marie's Little Cake Shop in

Auchterarder, Scotland. 'I think because I was star baker, people started asking me if I'd make cakes. And it got out of hand. My house was being overrun with cake stuff and my husband said did I want to find some premises?' She took a cake-decorating course at Peggy Porschen in Belgravia, and now specializes in wedding cakes. 'But you wouldn't believe it. I get people from the Highlands, from the Borders, from everywhere. They come for *Bake Off*, and they all want a wee selfie. A man came all the way from the Borders to buy cakes to take home. He said he wanted to sit down with his daughters, eat my cakes and watch *Bake Off*.'

John Whaite is now a fully-fledged TV presenter, co-hosting an ITV daytime show with Rosemary Shrager. Beca Lyne-Pirkis is also a TV star, with her own show on the Welsh language channel S4C, a job she juggles with being chef consultant at the foodies' paradise that is Borough Market. She is one of the busiest former bakers. 'I never dreamt going on would lead to this,' she says. 'I could pinch myself some days, to be honest.'

Ali Imdad presents a show on British Muslim TV and has a dessert parlour, Artisan, in Birmingham. 'Until *Bake Off* aired I just carried on with life as normal. Only once it airs do you get to gauge how it might affect your life, so that's when I decided to jump in the deep end. And I haven't looked back since. Having my own baking show is brilliant, because how many people get an outlet to show off their skills? Also, you don't get many male Muslim Asian bakers, so I get to play on that niche and it's just worked out great for me.'

Having a unique selling point also helps to secure a book deal. Chetna Makan took inspiration from India; Miranda Gore-Browne devoted her first book to biscuits; Holly Bell offered recipes 'from a normal mum'; and Howard Middleton went gluten-free (quote from Howard's website: 'My first cookbook is out now. . . And people actually like it!'). Ruby Tandoh may have mixed feelings – to put it mildly – about her time on *Bake Off*, but she has established herself as a respected food writer and author.

The life-changing nature of *Bake Off* isn't all about career opportunities, though. You only need to see Nadiya's newfound confidence to know that. Richard Burr now juggles his building work with writing cookbooks, giving demonstrations at cake shows and appearing on TV. The week he appeared on the BBC's *Saturday Kitchen*, he also spent refurbishing a house in Finchley. 'For someone who, when we got married, found the idea of doing a speech the most terrifying thing – to suddenly be thrust into telly stuff and demos was such an unfamiliar experience. But once I started doing it, I loved it. It has had an effect on every aspect of my life. I'm much more confident to tackle things without knowing there's going to be a positive outcome.'

Like most of the bakers, Richard does work for charities: in his case, volunteering at a local facility for people with eating disorders, helping at Great Ormond Street and raising funds for his local school. 'I'm not going to say that everything I do is mega-worthy – I do get to go to parties as well. But all of a sudden you've got this profile, and to be able to turn it into something good is a massive positive.' Oh, and he made a birthday cake for Zaire the gorilla at London Zoo (pro tip: if you're baking for a gorilla, put cashew nuts in your frosting).

Brendan Lynch visits retirement homes to get people baking, giving demonstrations and talking to residents about the food they loved. He believes in the therapeutic effects of baking.

Every *X Factor* finalist who goes out in the early rounds declares: 'This isn't the last you'll hear from me!' Before disappearing forever. But here again is where *Bake Off* is different, because post-show success is not dependent on how far a baker got in the contest. Stu Henshall, the musician who baked walnut cakes in between writing songs for The Prodigy, went out in the very first week of series six. But that brief appearance, and the column inches that went with it, have helped him to make a success of his business, The Alternative Kitchen. 'You get out what you put in,' he says. 'It gave me so many opportunities to do stuff with food. It's been an amazing experience.'

And Howard Middleton, eliminated in week six, thought he'd be going back to a job at Sheffield council. It was a conversation with Linda Hill, owner of Harptree Court, that made him think there might be more out there.

'I remember the week I went home, I was talking to the lady who owns the house and saying I was a bit sad now that it's all over. And she said, "But it doesn't have to be all over if you don't want it to be." And I thought, really? But I have been really fortunate.' He took voluntary redundancy and never looked back. And he's still refreshingly, Howardishly modest about it all. 'The first time they ever filmed me at the auditions, I had to make a coffee cake and I couldn't get the scales to work at all. And maybe they just thought: this is gold. This man is so inept that we couldn't fail to have him on.'

*

The BBC had a last hurrah with a two-part *Bake Off* Christmas special – shot months in advance, with the bakers all wearing winter coats for their walk to the tent despite it being summer, and the production team having gone to considerable lengths to source some Christmas trees. It featured eight of the fans' favourites: Howard, Chetna, Mary-Anne, Ali, Cathryn, James, Janet and Norman. Howard had forgotten to bring a coat, so had to borrow one from a member of the production crew. Norman – and who would expect anything less – threw himself

into proceedings with gusto, and appeared on screen bundled up in a scarf and trapper hat.

The last of the specials was followed by a little video that summed up all we loved about *Bake Off*. It featured all the highlights: Selasi's smile, Ruby's tears, Iain binning his Baked Alaska, an emotional Mary describing Nadiya's win as 'sheer perfection'. It faded out to Dean Martin's *Memories are Made Of This*. No, *you're* crying now.

A few months later, it was time for Channel 4 to give fans the first glimpse of the new series. The colourful teaser trailer featured slow-motion baked goods singing to the strains of everybody's favourite Paul McCartney track, *We all Stand Together* (featuring the Frog Chorus). There was even a welcome cameo from the Bread Lion.

And in no time at all, we were back in that famous tent. *Bake Off*, how we'd missed you.

Despite the glittering prizes, the endless column inches and the huge ratings, the show has never strayed far from its roots. The later series might be slicker than the first, the bakers more accomplished, but the main ingredients have remained intact: a family show with a warm, gooey centre. And a whole lot of cake.

Maybe the last word should go to a baker from the very first series, Miranda Gore Browne, who signed up for a show the world knew nothing about and became part of a great British phenomenon. How to explain why we took this programme to our hearts? 'Cooking is about food,' she says. 'Baking is about love.'